D1176409

BRIDGES

BRIDGES

Ministering to Those Who Question

David B. Ostler

GREG KOFFORD BOOKS
SALT LAKE CITY, 2019

Copyright © 2019 David B. Ostler
Cover design copyright © 2019 Greg Kofford Books, Inc.
Cover design by Loyd Isao Ericson

Published in the USA.

All rights reserved. No part of this volume may be reproduced in any form without written permission from the publisher, Greg Kofford Books. The views expressed herein are the responsibility of the author and do not necessarily represent the position of Greg Kofford Books.

ISBN 978-1-58958-726-7 (paperback)
Also available in ebook.

For additional resources visit http://www.bridgeslds.com

Greg Kofford Books
P. O. Box 1362
Draper, UT 84020
www.gregkofford.com
facebook.com/gkbooks
twitter.com/gkbooks

Library of Congress Control Number:2019944874

As I look back on my years of Church service, I realize that there are many who unnecessarily suffered because I didn't know how to effectively minister. I didn't know how to comfort them in their challenges, I didn't know how to mourn with them. To them, I offer this book, asking for their forgiveness. And since I am still learning, I ask for forgiveness of the mistakes of effort and understanding that I will yet make.

Contents

Introduction: Bridges,   ix

Section 1: A Crisis of Faith,   1

1. A Different Time,   3
2. How Societal Changes Affect Belief,   17
3. Why People Leave,   27
4. Confronting Today's Challenges of Faith,   47
5. How Faith Changes,   61

Section 2: Trust, Belonging, and Meaning,   73

6. Trust,   75
7. Belonging,   85
8. Meaning,   93

Section 3: Ministering,   101

9. Key Principles of Ministering,   103
10. Ministering at Church,   127

Conclusion: Not Walking Alone,   157

Appendix: Recommended Resources,   161
Notes,   165
Index,   179

Bridges

This book is about us—not about us and them. We are unified as members of The Church of Jesus Christ of Latter-day Saints, even though sometimes we may have differing kinds of faith. For some of us, our belief feels easy and complete. We believe all the principles taught in Church settings, have a strong testimony, and find deep meaning in Church teachings and doctrines. Others of us lack certainty but have confidence and hope in the gospel. And for some of us, our faith has changed, and we no longer believe as we once did—or even at all. Despite these differences, we are all Saints trying our best to find happiness and meaning in our lives and to be accepted and serve and love those around us.

I wrote this book primarily for those of us who believe, so we can better understand those of us who struggle to believe and those who struggle to maintain belief. A gap in understanding often separates believers and those classified as nonbelievers or doubters. When that gap is wide, it is more difficult to minister, show compassion, or mourn with those who mourn. As a result, those of us who don't believe as we once did suffer, experiencing loneliness and a sense of not belonging. But understanding why some of us have lost our faith helps to create a bridge and allows us to reach and minister to our brothers and sisters.

I have a strong testimony of our Heavenly Parents and our Savior Jesus Christ. From a young age I knew that they cared about me and knew who I was and what was in my heart. The gospel of Jesus Christ has been a natural part of my life. I try and base my life on the principles taught by the Savior, and although I have made my mistakes, I have peace knowing that the Savior's Atonement makes it possible for me to change and provides healing for those parts of me that are broken and sick.

I have family and friends who no longer believe in the doctrines that I hold dear. It hurts. I love them and want them to value what I believe and hope to be true. Because of these feelings, I have tried to understand why they no longer believe. I have asked them, listened to their reasons, studied social science, read religious history, and studied scripture and the words of our current Church leaders. I have conducted surveys of members, leaders, and those who no longer believe. I have read articles, books, and other material by Latter-day Saint writers, including Patrick Mason, Terryl and Fiona Givens, Adam Miller, Bruce and Marie Hafen, and others.[1] Many of the works I've read are directed to those who are currently experiencing a crisis of faith. This book, on the other hand, is for those who in one way or another strive to minister to those who are struggling with belief.

In this book, I use the term *faith crisis* to describe the state of dissonance and distress that some may experience regarding their belief in the Church and its teachings due to some sort of traumatic church event—including discovering new information about the Church that conflicts with their own understandings, disagreeing with a Church policy or doctrine, or having a difficult encounter with a Church leader. The usual result of such a crisis is the loss of faith in some or all of the foundational truth claims of the Church. Often the person who experiences a faith crisis was a fully believing member, a temple recommend holder, a returned missionary. They are thrown into disarray, completely unsure what they believe.

In the course of writing this book, I talked with a bishop who encountered the effects of a faith crisis during his first year of conducting tithing settlement interviews. Meeting with a stalwart couple, he thanked them for their service. In response, the couple awkwardly said, "Bishop, we have decided to leave the Church." The bishop was shocked. He had no idea that they had been struggling with their belief; it was a faith crisis that had triggered their decision. They, their children, and all their future descendants were now alienated from the Church. Their decision to leave may have caused those they served or served with to also question the Church.

I began studying the root causes of why people no longer believe while I was serving in a calling in our stake. Working under the direction of our stake presidency, my wife and I served for eighteen months as Church service missionaries. Our calling was to work with the almost one thousand singles in our stake. (This assignment excluded those in the local single wards, since they were in other stakes.) About 80 percent of our stake's singles were not attending church. We sent a letter to each of the nonattending singles, asking them to tell us why they no longer participated. They could complete an anonymous online survey, call us, or send us text or email messages. We told them we wouldn't preach to them; we just wanted to listen and to better understand why they no longer attend. Although the response rate was low, we learned that many felt that Church leaders didn't understand their concerns and situations. Combined with external research, we brought this information back to stake and ward leadership to help them in their ministering efforts. We realized that there are few resources available to local leaders to systematically understand Latter-day Saint disaffiliation, nonattendance, and loss of belief.

To augment our locally collected data, in May 2018 I conducted the *Local Leader Survey*[2] to better understand stake and ward leaders' perceptions of why people stopped believing. In September 2018, I conducted the *Faith Crisis Member Survey*,[3] this time of members who identified as being in a faith crisis. These surveys were not done in our stake, but nationally, with even some international responses. As the endnotes describe, these surveys are not statistically representative as such surveys would be extremely difficult or virtually impossible to conduct, but even with their limitations they provide provocative insights into key issues and concerns regarding modern day faith. In addition, I created the *Faith Crisis Member Focus Group*[4] where I could lead discussions on aspects of Latter-day Saint faith. I also interviewed about forty members and local leaders about faith crises and their experiences. I use many of their stories and comments in this book. Through all this research, I came to four major conclusions:

1. Ward and stake leaders could better understand members experiencing a faith crisis. Leaders frequently lack insight into both the issues leading to faith challenges and the pain, loss, and isolation these faith challenges can produce. This lack of understanding makes it more difficult for leaders to help members who are struggling to believe.

2. Ward and stake leaders recognize the need to address faith challenges but say they would value training on *how* to address them. They often have no tools or training to minister to those with faith challenges.

3. Because we as members and local leaders frequently don't understand these challenges, Church members experiencing a crisis of faith are largely unwilling to share their concerns and often appear to their families, ward members, and ward leaders to be completely believing. This can make it difficult to recognize how common faith challenges are among members.

4. Because leaders, members, and family members lack understanding of those facing faith challenges, those working through a faith crisis often feel unnecessary pain and disconnection. They work through their faith crisis alone, without an understanding and helpful minister by their side. If they do share belief concerns with others, they are often met with defensiveness, criticism, or judgment. Feeling isolated and unwelcome, many leave completely.

This last point may be surprising—at least it was to me. Many of us think about the pain we feel when a loved one no longer believes. I have certainly felt it. But as I talked with those who no longer believe, I learned that they also feel a great depth of pain. The issues they face sometimes challenge everything they have ever believed, turning their entire world upside down. Their faith crisis threatens their relationships with family members and sometimes (especially in the American Intermountain West) with their colleagues at work and with those in the community. In some cases, the reaction of leaders, Church members, and family members to their faith crisis inadvertently pushes them further away, making it harder for them to participate in the Church at all. Some become angry and bitter. Some reject it all.

We can't control how others feel, nor should we try, but by better understanding these faith challenges, we can more effectively minister and show love. Building a bridge requires humility and openness; we must open ourselves to the people we are trying to understand and put ourselves in their shoes, sincerely trying to see their perspective. Building a bridge means that we listen—not to formulate the perfect response, but to empathize, comfort, mourn, validate, and love. Building a bridge requires vulnerability, because our efforts may not always be reciprocated—there may be no one else building the other side of the bridge. But we keep learning and trying because of our love for them and our love for our Heavenly Parents.

At the Waters of Mormon, Christ's followers were baptized and promised that they would mourn with those who mourned and comfort those who stood in need of comfort (Mosiah 18:8-11). Without striving to understand the underlying reasons why people stop believing, we can't express the full love of our Savior and comfort them and mourn with them. This is why I decided to write a book for believing members—to help us better understand how to show compassion and love and to preserve relationships with those who struggle with their faith.

Bridges are meant to be crossed back and forth. While our efforts may seem in vain at times, building a bridge of compassion and understanding preserves our relationships and gives us a pathway for showing our love. Although we hope that those who have left will find belief again, we understand that may not happen, and yet we still build our bridge by working to understand. That bridge allows us to feel and express empathy and love, "that [they] may know that [our] faithfulness is stronger than the cords of death" (D&C 121:44).

My education and career were spent using data to improve the effectiveness of healthcare. I learned that the best decisions are those that are informed. So at times in this book, I will step back from my personal feelings and look at data from the best sources I can find, including external research by sociologists, research I have personally conducted, and analyses by professionals in religion, history, and philosophy in order to provide an objective, dispassionate, and at times unsparingly honest view of current challenges those in the Church are experiencing. Truly understanding the matters affecting faith requires a frank and honest discussion; without it, we may gloss over these issues and rationalize away their significance.

As I have read other authors on this subject, I have sensed that many have felt the same conflict—a conflict between a desire to be honest about the things that challenge faith and a desire to not discourage faithful members. We may worry that talking about difficult issues will give some in the Church reason to stop believing. I believe, however, that when we directly talk about difficult issues, not only do we increase our understanding, but we also better see how God's work moves forward. For example, when we directly and honestly confront challenges of our past, including our mistakes, we gain greater insight into and appreciation for the perfection of our Savior and God's mercy in having us, full of limitations, be coworkers in His work. Openness gives us opportunities for new insights, helping our faith grow. In this book, I have chosen to address challenging issues directly to help us build faith and confidently address these subjects with our families and friends and those we have stewardship over in our leadership roles.

For two people to communicate effectively, they need to use words the other understands. The Book of Mormon tells us that the Lord speaks "according to their language, unto their understanding" (2 Ne. 31:3). The Latter-day Saint historian and author Richard Bushman writes,

> Words are our entry into another culture. They are the way we make ourselves intelligible in a strange land. They not only allow us to connect, but to make ourselves understood. They show respect. We are making an effort to communicate in a way that can be understood. If we insist on using standard church language, we are in effect declaring our indifference.[5]

I have written this book using words that will hopefully be understood, that are meant to help the reader enter the culture of those who have stepped away from the Church. They think and feel differently than they once did, and because they are different than they were before, they often hear words differently.

***

This book is divided into three sections. Section 1, "A Crisis of Faith," discusses why many of our members are experiencing a crisis of faith and how changes in society have created a unique environment in which people, including those raised in the Church, are leaving the faith of their youth, perhaps more than at any other time. I share stories and data that illustrate the reasons behind this occurrence. Section 2, "Trust, Belonging, and Meaning," illustrates that unbelief largely stems from one of three reasons (or sometimes all three): losing trust in the Church or its leaders, not feeling a sense of belonging in the Church community, or not finding meaning or relevance in the doctrines of the gospel. Section 3, "Ministering," outlines the principles by which members and leaders, in both their families and wards, can build trust, create belonging, and help ourselves and others find meaning in Church doctrines and the gospel. By following these principles, we can create an environment that will help us retain and develop a stronger and more durable faith. All of the suggestions in this book are within the bounds of current Latter-day Saint standards of practice, as outlined in the Church handbooks, the teachings from our general leaders, and the scriptures.

I have deep spiritual feelings about these issues. They affect my family and those I love; they have caused me more sleepless nights, moments of pleading with my Heavenly Father, and anguish than any other event in my life. I am deeply committed to the Church and its powerful Christ-centered teachings, and I love the way members can change their lives by following Christ and the Church's teachings. And it's because of this commitment that I want to find a way to help all of us minister to those who are struggling with their faith. If you are a believer, I hope that reading this book will help you build your bridges with better understanding as you minister to those who doubt. If you consider yourself a doubter or nonbeliever, I pray that reading this book will give you hope that we are trying to be more understanding and that your relationships with family members, friends, and Church members can be strong and rich, even with differences in belief. Perhaps this book will help you find belonging and meaning, even without your former belief.

Without bridges we can't cross the gaps that divide us and we are unable to experience new lands and experiences. The Atonement is the eternal bridge that makes it possible for us to return to our Heavenly Parents. And that bridge is only possible because the Savior took upon Him all our sins and infirmities that He might know us and heal us (Alma 7:11; 3 Ne. 9:13). Because of His Atonement and with His help, we can also come to truly know our sisters and brothers and be His hands in bringing healing to those around us, succoring the weak, lifting up the hands that hang down, and strengthening those with feeble knees (D&C 81:5).

SECTION 1

A CRISIS OF FAITH

Our day is a day of unparalleled change. This is not just in the rapid pace of technology or inventions, the way we consume and access information, or the dynamic way our relationships have evolved. The change seems to be to life itself. We see it in our jobs, in the fields we have studied, and in politics. It's also in how we interact with one another, through electronic messaging and social media. The change is in society and in our relationships with families and our friends. And perhaps more significantly for Latter-day Saints, these changes affect how we think about God, religion, and our spirituality. Today is a different day.

CHAPTER 1

A Different Time

Compassion asks us to go where it hurts, to enter into the places of pain, to share in brokenness, fear, confusion, and anguish. Compassion challenges us to cry out with those in misery, to mourn with those who are lonely, to weep with those in tears. Compassion requires us to be weak with the weak, vulnerable with the vulnerable, and powerless with the powerless. Compassion means full immersion in the condition of being human.
—Henri Nouwen[1]

Almost all of us have a family member or close friend who was raised in the Church but, as an adult, no longer believes.[2] Having an authentic and loving relationship with these individuals means we must better understand what they are going through so that we are able to comfort and mourn with them as they struggle through a faith crisis. That is why we must build a bridge of understanding—so that we can show our love and compassion. When engineers design a bridge, they study the geology and subsurface conditions of the area, design a foundation, select the building materials, and create the supports that will bear the load between the two sides. Likewise, we begin our study by analyzing today's faith terrain so that we can understand the load that our bridge must carry.

People Leaving the Church in the United States Today

Many have sensed that persons leaving organized religion is a growing trend in the United States, even among those in the Church. Although we may be aware of the overall decline in religion in the Western world, we may wonder how that trend applies to the Church specifically. Available official Church data don't answer this question since membership records capture overall membership numbers but do not measure whether someone with a membership record still identifies as being a member of the Church.

Fortunately, there are surveys and sociological data that shed light on the current situation of religion in general, and of the Church in particular. In this book, I use data from Darren E. Sherkat (a professor of sociology who studies religion-related topics),[3] the Pew Research Center,[4] and recent studies done by Latter-day Saint scholars Jana Riess and Benjamin Knoll.[5] These resources are insightful and helpful to understanding the challenges of creating a durable faith in today's world and to responding to Latter-day Saints who no longer believe or practice in a traditional way.

In 2014, Sherkat published his analysis of religious affiliation for major religions within the United States, including Latter-day Saints. He identifies three measures that point to an increasing number of people leaving their faith:

1. **Religious loyalty:** the rate at which adults keep the religion they had when they were sixteen.

2. **Religious apostasy:** the rate at which adults leave the religion they had when they were sixteen and who presently have no religion.

3. **Gains and losses from switching:** a measure of the overall change in membership numbers, adjusting for converts coming in and those who leave.[6]

All denominations that Sherkat studied show similar trends, but they are more pronounced for Latter-day Saints: "Mormons . . . have high rates of loyalty in generations born before 1971, but in the youngest cohorts, loyalty drops to 61% and ranks Mormons among the least loyal groups in the youngest generation."[7] In that younger age group, Latter-day Saints have the highest rate of religious apostasy and the largest net loss from switching of any studied religious groups.

Religious Loyalty, Apostasy, and Overall Change Among Latter-day Saints

	Birth Years				
	Before 1925	1925–43	1944–55	1956–70	1971–94
Religious Loyalty	75.8%	74.2%	72.4%	71.2%	61.2%
Religious Apostasy	4.8%	5.8%	9.7%	17.6%	27.1%
Gains and Losses from Switching	29.0%	25.0%	21.0%	2.0$	-28.0%

According to Sherkat's findings, adult religious affiliation among those raised in the Church and who were born between 1971 and 1994 is dramatically different from that of prior generations. They are much more likely to no longer identify as Latter-day Saints (or with any other religious institution). For this age group, the Church has not been able to attract enough converts to replace those who are leaving, with a net outflow of 28 percent.

Riess took Sherkat's raw data and reanalyzed it. She found that for millennials (those born between 1981 and 1994) religious loyalty drops to 46 percent. The sample size is small, however, and therefore we should be cautious about its interpretation.[8] Sufficient data haven't been collected yet that would allow us to study those born after 1994.

The Pew Research Center supports these conclusions with its recent study of US religions. In 2007, they found that 70 percent of those raised in the Church identify as Latter-day Saint as adults. In 2014, that number dropped, with only 64 percent of those raised in the Church identifying as such.[9] This is a substantial decline. With a large margin of error, Pew's data indicates that an estimated 360,000 adults left the faith between 2007 and 2014 in the United States.[10] That translates to about twenty-five members in each congregation.

Knoll and Riess studied members of the Church and identified that the age of disaffiliation has decreased with each of the last three generations. They reported:

> We can also briefly take a closer look at what age former Mormons tend to disaffiliate from their Mormon identities. Former Mormons were asked: "About how old were you when you stopped identifying as a member of the LDS Church?" Among all former Mormon respondents, the average age is 21. This does not vary much by age cohort, though there appears to be a trend for disaffiliation at younger ages: the average age of de-identification for former Mormons who are currently Millennials is 18.4, Generation X is 21.1, and those of the Boomer or Silent generation is 23.7. Clearly young adulthood is the age when most former Mormons leave the fold, regardless of what age they are now.[11]

Data from Church records show a slowing growth of Church membership in the United States because of declining birth rates and lower numbers of converts. Since 2007, congregational growth has also slowed; between 2007 and 2016 in the United States, membership increased 12.2 percent, but the number of wards and branches increased only 7.7 percent, implying a decline in activity.[12]

While these statistics are sobering, more important than these trends are the brother, daughter, spouse, or friend who no longer believes. They aren't a statistic—they are people we know and love. Whenever even one person leaves the Church, while respecting their choice, we rightly mourn. We are sad that those who leave don't see the meaning we do in the gospel's teachings. We are sad that they couldn't trust Church leaders, that they felt unwelcome, that their questions were not heard—that they feel the Church somehow failed them. We are devastated.

The terrain of faith today is different than it once was. Our bridge often fails and needs to be stronger to be able to carry heavier loads. Throughout our history, belief in God has been almost universal and, at least in Western society, almost everyone used to affiliate with a religion. But because of broad societal and generational changes, it's now different. Many are spiritual but not religious, and many just don't believe in God at all.

Everyone is different, and there is no single reason why someone who previously expressed a strong testimony in God, the restoration of Christ's Church, and prophetic leadership loses those beliefs. We live in a different time, which means we need to reexamine our thinking on why and how we should respond. Throughout this book, I will share with you real stories of people who have left the Church, of those who don't know what they believe, and of leaders and members who are trying to build a bridge to help those who doubt. I don't soften these stories. Some of them are hard to read and reflect the deep feelings involved. When I share these stories with other members of the Church, I find that some become defensive, dismiss the individuals' concerns as insignificant, or rush to explain away the concerns. I used to do that myself, but I have learned to listen, to better understand, and to have empathy. I have learned so much and as a result find myself better able to relate, love, and minister to others than I was once able to. I like the words of Stephen Covey, who wrote about the importance of listening. He says, "If I were to summarize in one sentence the single most important principle I have learned in the field of interpersonal relations, it would be this: Seek first to understand, then to be understood."[13] As you read these stories, remember the promises that were made at the Waters of Mormon to mourn with those who mourn and comfort those who stand in need of comfort. Even though we may not know these people personally, we can still imagine putting our arms around them and expressing the love that we know our Heavenly Parents feel for each of their children.

Not Just a Statistic: Personal Stories[14]

Mike

Mike is thirty-five and was raised in a caring Latter-day Saint home with wonderful parents. In his words, "I grew up in the Church in a very loving home. Mormonism was a huge and defining part of our family. My parents are so amazing. To say I grew up active in my youth is kind of an understatement." He recalls a night when he was fourteen years old and reading the Book of Mormon as a part of a seminary assignment: "I just felt so pumped and good about it and turned to my brother and said, 'You need to read this, it is amazing.' It was the first time that I felt God in the Book of Mormon."

He served a mission to a foreign country and described the experience as the best thing he has ever done in his life. He felt that he was a successful missionary in terms of doing the work, following the rules, and feeling close to God. His leaders must have thought he was a trustworthy and faithful missionary since he was called to serve as a leader and was the assistant to the mission president for the last seven months of his mission.

He married in the temple within a year of returning home, and together, he and his wife founded their family in the gospel. He completed his education, established his career, served in Church callings, and appeared to have the typical and ideal Latter-day Saint family—temple marriage, four kids, successful career, and full activity in their ward.

About two years ago, Mike's brother told him that he no longer believed in the Church. Mike loved and trusted his brother, knew that he was a good person, and wanted to better understand his concerns. For about a year, Mike researched his brother's concerns, starting with issues about Church history. Even with all his previous gospel study, Mike had never heard that Joseph Smith had introduced and practiced polygamy and polyandry, that he used a seer stone when translating the Book of Mormon, and that modern-day translations and analyses of the papyri used to create the Book of Abraham do not correspond with the text of Joseph Smith's translation of them. Mike studied Church-produced materials, including the Gospel Topics Essays and other materials from Church scholars, and he learned how others had dealt with these often-unknown historical events. Throughout his research, he avoided reading blogs and articles by former Latter-day Saints.

Speaking of this period of struggle, Mike said, "I had never read so much, prayed so much, and fasted so much." Prior to this time, he had been a dedicated member who defended, served, and sacrificed for the Church. During his crisis of faith, he began to feel that everything he stood for might be wrong. He described this period as a time of terrible loneliness, when what he was learning was reshaping everything he believed in—his entire foundation of faith. He felt he couldn't talk to anyone about his struggles, which was agonizing. He would sometimes muster the courage to talk to someone, but when he finally broached the subject with them, he would get shut down. He felt alone and isolated and sometimes angry, in part because so many of the things that he had held dear now seemed dead—he was going through a grieving process. When he described his anger during this period, he mentioned his anger with himself—he felt that he had given all his moral authority to his Church leaders. He was angry with an entrenched Church culture that didn't seem to listen to people who were different.

Mike remains a spiritual person and believes the Church has a lot to offer, but everything has changed for him. He believes God and Christ are real—a belief he says is beautiful and comforting—but acknowledges that he may be wrong. He no longer believes that the Church of Jesus Christ of Latter-day Saints is the only true church or that he can tacitly trust general Church leaders without reservation or suspicion. He does, however, still believe that the Church is a good place to learn about God. He still attends church meetings on Sundays and keeps the commandments, but he misses the connection he once had with Church members because of their shared doctrine and belief.

Though he attends church weekly, Mike doesn't feel he can fully express his feelings to his ward members and friends. He recently taught a lesson in Elders Quorum about ministering to those who go through a faith crisis. He didn't raise any controversial issues but was authentic about some of his feelings. He felt that his lesson was not well-received and that he would likely not be asked to teach again. Despite these feelings of loneliness and not belonging, Mike is trying to figure out how he fits into his ward community and is trying to connect to people through love and service.

Three weeks before my interview with him, Mike started reading the Book of Mormon again. He feels direction in it but doesn't believe in it the way he did prior to his faith transition. During our one-hour conversation, he told me, "It feels so good to be able to tell someone your story and have them just listen. For some people, if you can share your story and walk away from that conversation knowing the person loves you, it can be lifesaving. Because it can be a very dark place sometimes."

I left the conversation in tears.

Because we are taught the importance of daily personal spiritual activities—like praying and scripture study—to insulate us from spiritual challenges, we may be conditioned to rationalize Mike's experience away. We are prone to assume that his loss of traditional faith is due to him not reading his scriptures regularly, not saying his personal prayers, or that maybe there was some secret sin that caused him to lose the Spirit. Without attempting to understand him, we might just view and label him as a tare that needs to be separated from the wheat (Matt. 13).

If we dismiss Mike's story and assume some other explanation for his change in belief, we lose the opportunity to learn from his experience and to find ways to love, understand, and minister to him and people like him. I believe that Mike's story is sincere. His family and leaders all helped build his faith exactly as we would have hoped; he was active as a youth, had a strong testimony, served valiantly as a missionary, married in the temple, attended Church regularly, and served faithfully in the Church as an adult. And yet, somehow he ended up in crisis, alone, angry, and terrified of what he had learned. His bridge of belief was gone, and there was no one there to help.

Amanda

Amanda's story is similar to Mike's. She had the ideal Latter-day Saint upbringing, full of faith, testimony, and service. She served a mission and married in the temple. She has four children, and when I interviewed her, she was thirty-four. While detailing her past activity in the Church, she underscored her devotion, telling me, "It's hard to overstate how 100 percent in I was as a youth and young adult. I was so passionate and excited about the gospel and to be a member of the Church." Amanda described her testimony as a bundled package of several truth claims, including Joseph Smith as a prophet, the Book of Mormon as divinely translated scripture, modern prophets as spokespersons for God, and the Church as the only true and living restored Church of Jesus Christ.

Amanda believes she was taught that avoidance was the best way to deal with difficult issues. This message wasn't always overt—no one taught her a lesson on how to avoid difficult issues—but it was communicated culturally as others around her avoided difficult questions and discouraged unorthodox points of view. She was, however, explicitly taught to avoid anti-Mormon literature because of its corrupting influence. Thus, in order to be faithful, she put difficult issues on a shelf to be dealt with later. In hindsight, she recognizes that one of her first concerns developed when she was a Beehive and first learned about the race prohibition of the priesthood. That policy felt wrong, but she placed it on her shelf. Over time her shelf was soon occupied by other issues she encountered as a youth and into adulthood.

Two years ago, her shelf broke, and over a long period of reading, studying, praying, and ultimately grieving, she came to believe "that she could not reconcile certain doctrines and attitudes within the Church that were required of me to participate." She believes in God and a Savior, but not in one true Church. Yet she still wants to find love and grace. With her husband, she teaches her children about love, relationships, and goodness.

Amanda doesn't desire to deconvert anyone. She doesn't try and convince anyone else to see things the way she sees them. She knows that the Church blesses some lives and is grateful for the meaning and direction it provides members, especially her parents. She wishes we could give that meaning and direction back to her. She isn't willing, however, to go back to the time when she didn't look critically at her spirituality and her relationship with God.

One reason Amanda wanted to talk with me was because she sees her relationships as the most precious things in her life. Her faith transition has impacted, and at times harmed, almost all her relationships with her family and church-going friends. She is hopeful that by sharing her experience, she can help leaders and members understand how to create accepting and loving relationships with those around them, even if they have different beliefs.

The strained relationship that has caused Amanda the most pain is the relationship with her parents. Before she had her faith crisis, her mother told her that having a child leave the Church is the worst thing that could ever happen to her. She knows they are devastated because they believe, based on Church theology, that her leaving the Church will affect their relationship in eternity. She wants her parents to still trust that she is a good person, that she is still led by and connected to God, and that she will teach her children to love, be kind, and follow God. But she still feels their disappointment and reflects that perhaps it was asking too much for them to be proud of her. Toward the end of my interview with her, with tears, she asked for advice on what she could do. "It's been really hard. I want to have that relationship back."

The tissues were out again. I have children who don't believe—do they believe that about me? Have I done anything that would cause them to think I don't accept them or have confidence in them and the course they choose? Have I failed to reach out in a way to let them know how proud I will always be of them? I want them to know that no matter what they do or believe, I will love them completely and without reservation. I want to—I try to—even though my beliefs are different.

***

Most all of us have a brother, sister, adult child, or close friend who no longer believes or attends Church. Many are like Mike and Amanda, who served missions, were married in the temple, and served faithfully in their wards for years. These are just two stories from the dozens of people I have interviewed. Although the people I spoke with come from all ages, backgrounds, and experiences, there are a few common threads that appear throughout their stories: Many question the nature of the Restoration or prophetic leader, others feel that the culture of the Church is not welcoming and that people are judgmental, and some just no longer connect with the teachings and doctrines of the Church.

My experience listening to people explain why they no longer believe as they once did has led me to believe we need to examine how to build faith to be enduring, particularly addressing these fundamental challenges:

- There are difficult issues in the history of the Church that we are often tempted to avoid, considering them either unimportant or too dangerous to discuss. When these issues are discovered, members sometimes lose trust in the Church's leaders because they feel the Church has hidden or manipulated parts of its history.

- Although we recognize the limitations of our leaders, we often place them on an unrealistic pedestal. Believing that they receive clear and definitive revelation, we are sometimes inclined to delegate our decision-making to them. As a result, when some Church members realize their leaders may have made mistakes, they lose their belief and trust in these leaders.

- Our Church community often provides no faithful place where we can discuss these historical issues or other troubling topics. Members with doubt feel isolated and may look outside the Church for answers.

- We sometimes blame the person who has doubts and believe they have done something wrong to trigger the loss of faith.

- There are members who are active in the Church and outwardly appear to be completely believing, yet they silently struggle with their faith, lacking confidence that they will be met with compassion and understanding if they raise or try to discuss their concerns.

Ministering to Those Experiencing a Crisis of Faith

In May 2018, I conducted the *Local Leader Survey*, a survey I administered with LeadingSaints (www.leadingsaints.org), an online platform providing tools to help Latter-day Saint leaders. I asked stake and ward leaders to respond to 135 statements about their own faith and about the faith challenges they see in their wards and stakes. I received 514 qualified responses, 48 percent from women and 52 percent from men. The respondents were of a wide range of ages and geographic representation, including 13 percent from outside of the United Status. The results of the survey are shown below.

Do You Have People in Your Circle That Have Had or Are in a Faith Crisis?
(*Local Leader Survey*)

	Many	Few	One/Two	None
Child	64.4% - At least one child			35.6%
Immediate family member	12.2%	26.6%	32.0%	30.1%
Extended family member	17.2%	41.6%	22.4%	18.9%
Close friend	14.1%	43.9%	28.1%	14.3%
Any family member or friends	97.0%			3.0%
In your ward	22.9%	53.7%	18.5%	4.4%
In your priesthood or auxillary organization	12.1%	39.8%	22.4%	25.3%

According to this data, 64.4 percent of current local Church leaders in the United States have at least one child who has experienced a faith crisis. Among these leaders, over 95 percent knew of someone in their ward who experienced a faith crisis, indicating that leaders would likely greatly benefit from more training on how to minister to those experiencing challenges to their faith. And an astounding 97 percent know a friend or family member who has experienced a faith crisis, further emphasizing that this concern touches us all. I would love to go back in time and ask this question twenty or forty years ago. I suspect the data would be very different. In the 1990s, I served as a bishop and stake president. During that time I ministered to only a few people considering leaving the Church. We face a different challenge today.

Here are the results to another question:

How Important Do you Think It Is to Address Faith Crises in These Settings?
(Local Leader Survey)

	Very Important	Important	Unimportant
In church generally	67%	31%	1%
In my stake	60%	37%	3%
In my ward	65%	33%	2%
In my priesthood or auxillary organization	64%	32%	5%
In my family	76%	21%	3%

Based on the answers given to the first question—which indicate that knowing someone who has experienced doubt is near universal—it is not surprising that only a few believe that addressing faith crises is unimportant. And while over 67 percent of Church leaders surveyed felt that addressing faith crises in Church was very important, the highest percentage of respondents, at 76.2 percent, pointed to the family as a very important setting in which to address faith challenges. Given our love for our families and the Church's teachings on the sacred nature of the family, it is unsurprising that we seem to be most sensitive about faith within our families than within any other organization.

I also asked questions about whether leaders think they are receiving training about faith crises or have confidence in their or their ward's ability to minister to those in a faith crisis. Here are the findings:

Rate Each Statement about Faith Crises
(Local Leader Survey)

	Strongly Agree	Agree	Disagree	Strongly Disagree
The Church as a whole provides adequate information for leaders to help people who are in a faith crisis.	9.7%	43.4%	36.2%	10.7%
Our stake and ward provides training to leaders about faith crises.	1.6%	13.5%	55.8%	29.1%
My ward leaders know how to effectively minister to individuals in a faith crisis.	1.4%	25.1%	55.2%	18.4%
I feel that I can effectively help a person who is having a faith crisis.	8.5%	45.9%	38.8%	6.7%
I feel that I can effectively help my family members avoid having a faith crisis.	5.8%	43.7%	43.1%	7.4%

These results surprised me. Stake and ward leaders were somewhat ambivalent to the statement that the Church provides adequate materials to address faith challenges and to the statement that they feel able to effectively minister to those in a faith crisis. A full 85 percent disagreed or strongly disagreed that their wards and stakes provide training to leaders on faith crises, and almost 74 percent disagreed that their ward leaders know how to effectively minister to those doubting their faith. The vast majority of leaders believe that addressing faith challenges in church is very important yet indicate they are not receiving the training to help them do so. For me, the data indicates that something is different today than it once was: current local leaders worry and have a lack of confidence in how to respond to those struggling with their faith.

In September 2018, I administered my *Faith Crisis Member Survey* to members of a social media group of Latter-day Saints who are in a faith crisis but are working to remain positively engaged with the Church. I asked participants to respond to seventy-three questions and statements about them, their faith, and their understanding of a faith crisis. I received 320 responses that met the selection criteria of being in a current faith crisis; the respondents were of a wide mix of ages, gender, and geographic locations within the United States. Here are their responses:

Rate Each Statement about Faith Crises
(*Faith Crisis Member Survey*)

	Strongly Agree	Agree	Disagree	Strongly Disagree
The Church as a whole provides adequate information for leaders to help people who are in a faith crisis.	0.0%	.6%	25.9%	73.4%
Our stake and ward provides training to leaders about faith crises.	0.0%	.6%	38.4%	61.0%
My ward leaders know how to effectively minister to individuals in a faith crisis.	0.3%	3.8%	40.9%	55.0%

These responses are from the very members we are at risk of losing, and they have no confidence in materials from the Church, training within the stake and ward, and the ability of their leaders to understand and minister to their needs. If we are unable to understand them, I fear that these trends of disaffiliation will continue.

The Church is aware of these challenges and is responding. Faith challenges have always existed, but today's faith challenges are different and need new approaches. Elder Marlin K. Jensen said, "The [First Presidency and Quorum of the Twelve] really do know, and they really care. And they realize that maybe since Kirtland, we never have had a period of, I'll call it apostasy, like we're having right now."[15] Every general conference in recent years seems to have at least one address about strengthening faith. Some of my favorites are Elder Jeffrey R. Holland's April 2017 "Songs Sung and Unsung,"[16] President M. Russell Ballard's October 2016 "To Whom Shall I Go?"[17] and Elder Dieter F. Uchtdorf's October 2013 "Come, Join with Us"[18] and October 2014 "Receiving a Testimony of Light and Truth."[19]

The Church has also published the Gospel Topics Essays on its website that provide background information on historical and doctrinal topics that may be challenging for some members, including polygamy, the various accounts of the First Vision, the Book of Mormon translation, and teachings about women and the priesthood. Curriculum has been expanded to include additional resources that teachers can use to address concerns raised by class members. The Church's efforts to be transparent include monumental efforts by the Church History Department, including the Joseph Smith Papers Project (a remarkable endeavor to provide early Church documents to members and researchers)[20] and *Saints: The Story of the Church of Jesus Christ in the Latter Days* (the most complete and accurate history that has ever been published by the Church).

Beyond its efforts to be more transparent, the Church has introduced new types of instruction, including the *Come Follow Me* curriculum for youth, doctrinal mastery in seminary, first-Sunday council meetings, and curriculum for Relief Society and Elders Quorum that rely on discussions of general conference talks. Teacher council meetings now provide a setting for teachers to discuss ways to create unity in the classroom and teach about difficult issues.

With the retirement of the Home and Visiting Teaching programs and the introduction of their replacement, ministering, Church members are encouraged to move beyond monthly (and often mechanical visits) with other members to a more ministerial process. President Jean B. Bingham, the general president of the Relief Society, described ministering as a process of loving and informed service: "We ask, 'What does she [or he] need?' Coupling that question with a sincere desire to serve, we are then led by the Spirit to do what would lift and strengthen the individual."[21] Similarly, Elder Jeffrey R. Holland says,

> We have an opportunity as an entire Church to demonstrate "pure religion . . . undefiled before God"—"to bear one another's burdens, that they may be light" and to "comfort those that stand in need of comfort," to minister

to the widows and the fatherless, the married and the single, the strong and the distraught, the downtrodden and the robust, the happy and the sad—in short, all of us, every one of us, because we all need to feel the warm hand of friendship and hear the firm declaration of faith.[22]

These recent efforts by the Church are important and significant, but much of the work of ministry needs to be in our local congregations or outside of Church among our friends and in our families. We are the ones who can help build trust and create an environment of belonging where we can all find meaning from the gospel of Jesus Christ in our lives. As local Church leaders and members, we have opportunities to practice the "pure religion" Elder Holland references by reaching out in compassion and trying to understand those who question the Church and its teachings. We can build bridges in how we teach and in the space we create for those with differing views.

CHAPTER 2

How Societal Changes Affect Belief

Gone are the days when a student asked an honest question and a teacher responded, "Don't worry about it!" Gone are the days when a student raised a sincere concern and a teacher bore his or her testimony as a response intended to avoid the issue.
—President M. Russell Ballard[1]

Carly, a stake Relief Society president serving in another city, recently shared with me an experience she had. Her daughter, who had returned from her mission several months before, and eight of her friends from her previous Young Women group came over for a get-together. Three of the women who had served missions no longer believed in the Church. Carly didn't understand why, and she was surprised that their disaffiliation seemed so unremarkable to her daughter.

The same day I talked with Carly, I talked with Jacob, who had returned from his mission four months earlier. He wanted to help his uncle retain his belief in the Church—after all, during his two years as a missionary, Jacob had taught investigators and helped build their faith. But, as he heard his uncle's concerns about early Church history, Jacob started to doubt the Church himself, and now he doesn't know what he believes.

The Millennial Generation

What gives? Life and society are transforming—our values and the way we apply them, the way we affiliate with one another, and the way we see the world. The causes and trends of these changes are all interrelated but can perhaps best be seen by looking through the eyes of "millennials" (those born between 1981 and 1996) and the societal changes related to technology. Millennials, who are all now adults, came of age amidst the social changes of the last two decades and are the first to grow up surrounded by much of the technology we have today. Millennials tend to gather and process information differently than my generation, and they affect society more than one might think. According to the Pew Research Center, "America is in the throes of a huge demographic shift, and a major factor in this sea change is the millennial generation, which is forging its own distinct path to adulthood."[2]

As a baby boomer, I often hear people in my generation speak disparagingly of millennials. Some see them as lazy and unmotivated, living at home with their parents, without values or too inclined to move from new experience to new experience. However, like many stereotypes, these negative assessments don't hold up to critical examination. Millennials have strong values, but they apply them differently, which confuses us old folks. For example, my generation strongly values family—and the image of that family is one with a working husband, a stay-at-home wife and mother, and 2.5 children. Millennials also share strong family values, but those values tend to emphasize the importance of the relationship than an adherence to duty. Thus, partners in millennial couples are more inclined to share responsibilities with each other, both inside and outside the home, and are less likely to value career or money over time with family. Accordingly, they tend to marry later when they feel ready and have fewer children. They are more accepting of same-sex couples than previous generations, and as a result, gay millennials are more likely to be open about their romantic relationships. Millennials change jobs more frequently, and for them, changing jobs is often motivated by a desire to maintain a particular work-life balance or to find a company whose values correspond with their own.[3]

A full discussion of the changes and trends among the millennial generation is beyond my scope here, but worth noting are the profound differences between this generation and previous generations that impact faith. Millennials in America, for instance, are less attached to religion, with over 36 percent saying they don't affiliate with any religion. But, surprisingly, 46 percent say they pray daily, compared to only 40 percent of Gen-Xers and 41 percent of boomers. Millennials have traditional views on heaven and belief in God, but they are less inclined to find answers to their spiritual questions in church pews. Many millennials feel directed more by their emotions and personal beliefs than they do by the culture or religion in which they were raised. They are less likely to recognize the absolute moral authority of religious institutions or their leaders, and they are more likely to base their decisions on how they feel rather than what is expected of them.[4] (Hence, they are more concerned with marrying when and with whom it feels right, rather than out of an imperative to do so.)

Perhaps because the millennial generation is more ethnically and culturally diverse than previous generations, their values include issues of social and economic justice. They value inclusion more than any prior generation and tend to strongly advocate for social fairness, rejecting discrimination based on race, religion, gender, or sexual orientation. These are, of course, generalizations—there are millennial racists, sexists, and homophobes—but, overall, these trends hold. Riess's work on Latter-day Saint millennials supports these findings. She writes that "they also struggle with whether they will be able to . . . reconcile the tensions they feel between exclusivist claims and their generation's generally inclusive, tolerant and open-minded world-view."[5]

Trust is an important issue for millennials. Only 19 percent of millennials agreed that "most people can be trusted."[6] Their mistrust of individuals extends to institutions and political parties—they are more likely to be politically independent, for example. This generation is also the first to face higher rates of poverty and unemployment; this holds true even for college graduates, whose collective debt burden is significant.[7] On a brighter side, millennials, particularly women, are better educated, and their college graduation rates are higher than in any prior generation. Women's graduation rates are now higher than men's.[8] Millennial women work more,[9] marry later,[10] and have fewer children after they marry.[11]

Finally, when discussing millennials, we have to talk about selfies. The word "selfie" was added to the Oxford Dictionary in 2013 and embodies the broader, yet individually centered, world of today. The perfect picture focused on one's self reflects the increase of individualism in today's culture. And this individualism has a notable effect on religious observance, as one recent study discovered: "religious involvement was low when individualism was high in the society."[12] The study defined "individualism" as a result of a cultural system that focuses more on the self and less on social rules. The study concludes that when people are focused on themselves, they are less likely to affiliate with a religious group that has rules and less likely to unquestioningly follow leaders.

Technology

Of course, the rise of the selfie was made possible through our rapidly evolving technology that has had a profound effect on our culture and the way we find and digest information. Today we can find information instantly. The internet offers every kind of information—from when that rainstorm out in the distance will arrive to live webcam views of your favorite Costa Rican white-sand beach. When I was writing this paragraph, I did an internet Google search for "How many questions does Google get asked a day?" and in .66 seconds, I discovered that Google processes 40,000 questions per second and 3.5 billion every day. Importantly, it's not just teenagers and adults who are turning to the internet to find answers. Yesterday, I heard my seven-year-old grandson ask a virtual voice assistant, "Alexa, what is the temperature?" We ask and get answers. And because we get mostly reliable answers, we ask more questions.

Technology has made possible the rise of our on-demand world. We can browse an almost infinite number of movie titles and then stream them immediately, without ever leaving the couch. We hail rides using apps like Uber and Lyft, with only a five-to-ten-minute lead time. We can buy almost anything on Amazon.com and are disappointed if it takes more than two days to be delivered. Where my family lives, we can order groceries online or via an app after breakfast and have them delivered before lunch. So many things are just a click or a tap away.

Technology has also changed our social structures and the ways we associate with and make friends. A hundred years ago, we talked mostly with people who lived nearby and largely shared our own beliefs and experiences. We learned, prayed, studied, and socialized with our physical neighbors. When my wife and I moved from Utah to New Hampshire almost forty years ago, we left behind family and friends with the hope that we would develop new friends. It was expensive to call long distance, and casual air travel was relatively more expensive than it is today. We knew we would talk to our family only monthly and travel to see them just once every other year. We mailed letters with photographs as a way of connecting.

Today, travel is cheaper, young adults don't even know what a long-distance call is, and Instagram, Facebook, Skype, Messenger, Facetime, WhatsApp, and other technologies keep us continually in touch. With cheap transportation and job mobility, we can live or visit almost anywhere and interact with almost anyone. With the advent of the internet, we don't even have to move from our computer to find and talk with almost anyone who shares an interest or point of view. Now, we can join any number of online communities such as Facebook and Reddit and find others who share our interests and concerns. We no longer have the same necessity of fitting in or adapting to the physical communities, including religious communities, we live in.

In this on-demand world and with the rise of individualism and self-directed values, it has become easier to find instant and online communities that match our individual and unique social and spiritual values. We can build friendships and relationships as well as explore the questions and ideas that are important to us. Whether a person is interested in cats, sports, or spirituality, there seems to be a virtual community for everyone.

Switching Costs

On-demand services have lowered switching costs for consumers for many products and services. Switching costs are what consumers incur—whether it be of time, money, or effort—when they change what brands, suppliers, or products they use. Many companies try to make switching costs high by tying you to a contract (a gym membership), leasing you the underlying equipment (cell phone companies), creating loyalty programs (airlines with frequent-flyer programs), or trying to create unique products where there are limited options. Yes, there are monopolies that make switching impossible, but generally we have more choices about the products we use than we once did, and the more products and options we have, the more opportunities there are to switch.

We always evaluate the cost of switching. Sometimes we may pass on an opportunity to switch if we see the cost as being too high. For example, I use a Windows PC to write, access the internet, pay my bills, and do my taxes. I often look at my wife's Mac, with its lighter weight, handsome design, and simple interface and say to myself, "I really should get a Mac." But I know how hard it would be to move all my stuff over to a new computer, change programs, and learn a new interface. We base so many of our decisions on cost and reward, and for me, the cost of switching to a new computer is higher than the reward of having a sleeker and trendier computer with additional features. Of course, there are some people that just want change and will switch for the sake of switching, but most of us like stability.

The cost of switching is determined not only by the cost of money or effort but also by societal costs. As the societal costs go down, switching becomes easier and less disruptive to our lives. This applies not only for what we buy and consume but also for other aspects of our lives:

- **Marriage.** Even with a lower divorce rate among millennials,[13] divorce is much more common today. One reason for a higher divorce rate is that the cost of divorce is much lower. Society is more accepting of divorce, and women have more career options and economic freedom outside of marriage. In 1900, less than one in ten marriages resulted in divorce; in 1940 it was two in ten; in 1972 it was four in ten; the divorce rate has stabilized today at five in ten.[14]

- **Jobs.** One hundred years ago, people would likely spend their entire working lives in the same career and perhaps with the same company. Technology has virtually eliminated whole job categories, such as switchboard operators, travel agents, and insurance underwriters. Automation has impacted jobs everywhere, from the family farm to the manufacturer. Future changes are all but guaranteed, including changes in the fields of transportation (with self-driving cars, for instance), construction, and even professional fields such as law and medicine. Many are forced to change jobs because of these structural trends, but millennials are also more inclined to switch jobs because of their personal values and will switch for reasons related to corporate social awareness,[15] work-life balance, and family.[16] In doing so, people aren't just switching companies; they are often switching whole careers.

- **Political parties.** One hundred years ago, a person's identified political party as an adult was very likely to be the same political party of the family into which they were born. Choosing for themselves, individuals are now more likely to disassociate from the political party of their parents. Many choose to be independent, and in fact, today there are more independents than members of either of the two major political parties.[17]

And of course there is religion. Today, it is easier for individuals to leave formal religion entirely, and they are doing just that. More and more people are switching from a particular religious affiliation to no religious affiliation. This has been called by Pew the "Rise of the Nones." The decline in religious behavior isn't limited to Latter-day Saints. Almost every religion is experiencing a decline in individual affiliation. In the United States, between 2007 and 2014, adults who are religiously unaffiliated increased by 43 percent, from 16 percent of adults to 23 percent—a rather staggering increase in just seven years. While this overall rise is partly due to more millennial adults dissociating from organized religion, even for non-millennials, the level of religious commitment and affiliation significantly decreased in those same years.[18]

Maintaining Faith in the Information Age

One hundred years ago, if I wanted to find an answer to a difficult question, I would go to an expert or find a book. Now I can use Google to ask a question, read several possible answers, and then decide for myself which solution is right for me. If I have a difficult spiritual question and want to read what others thought about it, I likely wouldn't wait until Sunday to talk with a Church leader. I would Google it right now and sort through the potential results to see if anyone might help me. Maybe I would ask friends in an online community.

Of course, not all searches yield good results, and not all communities are helpful. But the internet is successful because it provides answers immediately and because we largely trust its results; we value answers from online friends because, having first sought them out because they were in some way like us, we trust them.

The immediacy of what the internet offers, however, may provide a naïve sense of assuredness from persons on both sides of the religious divide—such as trying to find a reliable answer to a complex question like "Was Joseph Smith a prophet?" Questions of faith are often subjective and need to be answered on a personal level. While talking to others and reading about others' experiences may be helpful, trying to find quick and reliable answers on the internet can be difficult and fruitless. Some questions don't have answers, and some search results require careful reading and interpretation, tasks not usually done in today's on-demand world. Some things, like faith, take time. Some answers don't come immediately, and some don't come at all. Others only find resolution through pondering, prayer, patience, and meditation. Our faith stretches and changes throughout our lives. Having the patience and persistence, however, to ponder through faith-related questions is harder now in a time of next-day delivery.

Some may argue that we shouldn't look to the internet when learning about Church history and spiritual matters. After all, there are critics of the Church and online communities that actively spread the message that the Church is a fraud. Those who preach avoidance likely have seen loved ones lose trust in the Church and its teachings after encountering unflattering information about a Church leader or some aspect of Church history for the first time online. Those who want to avoid online sources (or limit sources to only those that have been created by the Church) are right to be concerned. With the availability and ubiquity of information available through the internet, however, it's not realistic to believe that the Church can control access to discussions surrounding tough topics. People will Google the things that are important to them and will then decide what results to trust.

Technology has its place in helping maintain faith. The Church's recent efforts to change curriculum and increase the transparency and availability of its history all indicate that Church leaders want to help us respond to faith-related challenges. In an address to CES teachers, President Ballard demonstrated an understanding that our teaching needs to be more effective at addressing challenging issues:

> As Church education moves forward in the 21st century, each of you needs to consider any changes you should make in the way you prepare to teach, how you teach, and what you teach if you are to build unwavering faith in the lives of our precious youth.
>
> Gone are the days when a student asked an honest question and a teacher responded, "Don't worry about it!" Gone are the days when a student raised a sincere concern and a teacher bore his or her testimony as a response intended to avoid the issue. Gone are the days when students were protected from people who attacked the Church. Fortunately, the Lord provided this timely and timeless counsel to you teachers: "And as all have not faith, seek ye diligently and teach one another words of wisdom; yea, seek ye out of the best books words of wisdom; seek learning, even by study and also by faith.". . .
>
> For you to understand the doctrinal and historical content and context of the scriptures and our history, you will need to study from the "best books," as the Lord directed. The "best books" include the scriptures, the teachings of modern prophets and apostles, and the best LDS scholarship available.[19]

Because the faith challenges of many individuals stem from feelings of being lied to or deceived, these steps toward transparency are positive and will help build trust in the Church and its leaders.

But it's not realistic, or perhaps even good, to try and control access to information and opinions about something as important as our foundational religious and spiritual beliefs. People today are more educated and less trusting of institutions and leaders. They are more inclined to sort through information and make their own choices about what they believe, often favoring authenticity and sincerity. In the process of information gathering, it is inevitable that individuals will be exposed to potentially challenging issues regarding the Church.

Mike, whose experience was briefly discussed in the previous chapter, says that as a youth, missionary, and adult Church leader, he never learned that Joseph Smith practiced polygamy. One night, prompted by his brother, he Googled, found authoritative sources, and learned what he hadn't been taught in seminary. He didn't have to go to a library; he didn't have to talk to a historian; it was right there instantly at his fingertips. Somehow, we failed him when at age thirty-four he learned about it for the first time and with no faith-based framework for understanding it. He felt Church leaders had hid the information because they knew it would potentially undermine the message of the Restoration. Then, when he learned about Joseph translating through seer stones, he concluded that there was a pattern of covering up our history. In a day with less trust, he lost confidence that the Church would teach the truth. He questioned what else might be different from what he was taught.

Gone are the days when we can control how our history is told.

Gone are the days when our members only have access to Church-published materials.

Gone are the days when it is uncommon to find Church members who have questions about Church history or policy.

Gone are the days when it can be assumed that members share an unreserved trust in Church leaders and the institutional Church.

It's a different day. Young people, like they have in the past, are influencing society—its values, media, and culture. With these societal changes, the rise of individualism, the decline of institutional authority, and immediate access to information, our time is now different. We need new ways to discuss faith, which stand against these trends. In later chapters, we will see how Church members have used prophetic words, new materials, and new approaches to teaching and ministering to respond to the challenges of today.

CHAPTER 3

Why People Leave

One might ask, "If the gospel is so wonderful, why would anyone leave?"
Sometimes we assume it is because they have been offended or lazy or sinful.
Actually, it is not that simple. In fact, there is not just one reason that applies
to the variety of situations. Some of our dear members struggle for years with
the question whether they should separate themselves from the Church.
—Elder Dieter F. Uchtdorf [1]

Understanding the ground on which we must build a bridge is a first step, but to truly know how to connect to others and bridge the gap between ourselves and those who doubt, we must seek to understand why people struggle with their faith. For some readers this may be a heavy chapter. It can feel like a ton of bricks crashing down just reading about all the reasons that persons may struggle with faith. I have studied, prayed, and even fasted to know how frank I should be in helping readers understand the challenges some face. I have chosen to be direct, and I realize this approach may trigger questions or even spark doubt for those who might be learning about various issues for the first time. But I see no way of understanding the reasons why someone would stop believing without talking about these issues directly.

Our genetics, culture, and life choices make each of us unique—none of us is the same. When individuals decide to leave the Church or when their faith changes, their reasons for doing so are as unique as they are. Too often we assume that these individuals weren't valiant, didn't keep the commandments, or didn't read the scriptures or pray. But to nurture positive relationships based on respect and empathy we need a bridge of understanding—that is, we need to understand from their perspective why people are struggling and leaving the Church. [2]

Ultimately belief comes from what we experience and how we feel. Within the Church, we call these feelings and experiences testimonies and spiritual impressions. I regularly reflect on a time, just before my mission, when I was backpacking with a close, lifelong friend. Up in the mountains, looking at the stars, I felt God. I knew that He knew me. I knew that He had a hand in my life. That thought is not the only part of my belief, neither was that experience my only spiritual experience; it's one of many that I regularly remember and am grateful for. Without testimony, we have no belief.

Beyond personal testimony, I have found that there are three attributes that, if achieved, have a positive effect on one's belief and participation in church. I will explore these topics in depth in Section 2, but I briefly introduce them now, alongside personal statements of what a Church member should be able to say if they feel each of the three attributes.

- *Trust.* Even with the limitations of Church members and leaders, I have confidence that the Church and its leaders will help me find spiritual purpose and guidance. I trust leaders and other members to help me as I make choices for my own spiritual growth.

- *Belonging.* My ward accepts my authentic self and supports me as I develop my own spirituality and relationship to God. I feel like I belong and feel love, acceptance, and support—even with my differences.

- *Meaning and relevance.* I feel spiritually lifted when I think of Church doctrines and participate in the Church. I feel my most important questions are addressed and answered. I feel closer to my Heavenly Parents and find meaning and direction in the teachings and doctrines of the Church.

Modern challenges in the Church impact these three attributes in ways not previously experienced. Although individuals, including those not experiencing a faith crisis, leave the Church for their own unique and individual reasons, there are a few issues that crop up repeatedly. Below, I describe those things that sometimes trigger individuals to lose their sense of meaning, trust, or belonging in the Church.

Church History

In the *Faith Crisis Member Survey,* I asked, "How much do questions about Church history contribute to an individual's faith crisis?" Eighty-four percent responded that Church history strongly contributes, and another 16 percent responded that it contributes. In fact, Church history was the largest contributor, with all respondents identifying Church history as a contributor to their faith challenges.

In the twentieth century, as the Church grew and responded to an increasingly international membership, it created a standardized narrative of its history and beliefs. In the 1996 publication *Our Heritage: A Brief*

History of The Church of Jesus Christ of Latter-Day Saints, our almost 190 years of Church history were condensed into only 146 pages.[3] The book is simple and easy to read, and as intended, it builds faith. But, it makes no mention of some of the more difficult issues that members may face in our history, including the Mountain Meadows Massacre, Joseph Smith's practice of polygamy, or the origins of the priesthood ban. These are difficult issues, and it isn't surprising that they wouldn't be included in a publication meant to introduce the history of the Church to members and nonmembers alike. But even in the current version of the teacher's manual for adult Sunday School classes on the Doctrine and Covenants and Church history, there is no mention of Mountain Meadows, only a brief reference that Joseph practiced polygamy, and nothing about the origins of the priesthood ban.[4]

In 2018, the Church published *Saints: The Story of the Church of Jesus Christ in the Latter Days: The Standard of Truth: 1815–1845*.[5] The writing of the book is very accessible, and it includes relatively unknown stories and events, the voices of women, and issues that were largely unknown or rarely discussed in other Church publications, including Joseph Smith's polygamy and the secrecy that surrounded it, as well as the use of seer stones in the Book of Mormon translation and the prevailing culture of folk magic that Joseph came from. The book is a remarkable effort toward being open about our early history.

These issues aren't new and have been discussed since they happened. But what *is* new is that with the internet and social media, many members who aren't even looking come across these historical topics outside of church, and sometimes outside of settings where they can be discussed in a faithful way. These topics are discovered through internet searches and online communities and through family or friends. Today, the Church is much more transparent and forthcoming about its history, but for many members, this effort has come too little too late—many adults today who did not grow up with this information may become distressed when they first learn of these things.

In a comment from the *Faith Crisis Member Survey*, one woman wrote, "Trust—I have a very hard time trusting the Church because of the many times I was lied to about Church history." This statement can be hard to hear, but I have heard it again and again.

As mentioned before, the Church has undertaken a remarkable effort to be more transparent in its history, and I am hopeful these new materials will be incorporated into future curriculum and that teachers will not shy away from teaching them. One way that the Church has addressed difficult issues of history and policy is through the Gospel Topics Essays, which were published online starting in 2013. These essays, however, have been given only limited introduction to general Church membership, with just brief or optional references in established curriculum, general conference, or training materials. In the *Local Leader Survey,* I found that 25 percent of female leaders and 9 percent of male leaders hadn't even heard about the Gospel Topics Essays, and only 42 percent of female leaders and 66 percent of male leaders have read more than one or two of them. I suspect that the general membership is even less familiar with them.

Leaders surely know that these essays and other materials can come with difficult tradeoffs. On the one hand, they don't want to create distrust in the Church by exposing people to these challenging topics, but they also want this information to be available, both to provide transparency and to provide a faithful perspective and interpretation of its history, with all its limitations, for those concerned about our past.

Some of the topics that *Saints* and the Gospel Topics Essays address are difficult, and these sources won't always resolve readers' concerns. One woman commented in the *Faith Crisis Member Survey,* "I had mostly stopped attending church by the time [the essays] were published. I was legitimately excited and really hoped that they would contain at least a few of the answers I'd been searching for. Instead I felt like I was failed again. I literally cried because I realized that those concerns I had were never going to be answered." There aren't answers to all questions. History as a discipline doesn't just identify facts, it also places those facts in context so they can be interpreted. In that process, historians can take the same historical events and interpret them differently. Even the essays can lead readers to different conclusions regarding the events of the past and especially regarding spiritual belief.

Church LGBTQ Policies and Practices

Some Church members are unable to reconcile their personal beliefs about LGBTQ (lesbian, gay, bisexual, transgender, and queer) individuals with the Church's policies and practices that affect them. Though society has become drastically more accepting of gay marriage and gay relationships over the years, polarization remains. And unfortunately, it is still common, even in the Church, to hear unkind, hurtful, and prejudiced comments about those who are gay, bisexual, or transgender. We also face complicated issues both inside and outside the Church regarding gender identity. These issues are complex, and in just my lifetime we have seen several high profile or controversial events involving LGBTQ issues that the Church has been involved in. Today, the Church has moved away from its support of conversion and electroshock therapy and no longer teaches that being gay is the result of inadequate parenting or that same-sex attraction in itself is sinful. However, with its commitment to "traditional" families, the Church has also been involved in political initiatives advocating for the rejection of gay marriage and restriction of rights for LGBTQ citizens through numerous legislative, legal and citizen actions,[6] including Proposition 8 in California in 2008. For some members, this has been difficult. Likewise, the November 2015 policy preventing children with a parent in a same-sex relationship from being baptized and labeling those in a gay marriage as apostates was difficult for many members. Although the Church reversed its policy in March 2019, many members remain hurt, alienated, and angered by the Church's original policy and confused as to the prophetic role, first in its creation and then its reversal.

In the *Faith Crisis Member Survey*, I asked, "How much does the Church's LGBTQ policy contribute to an individual's faith crisis?" I left the interpretation of this question up to the respondent. Eighty-two percent responded that it strongly contributes, with another 17 percent responding that it contributes. That's 99 percent. Women had the most intense feelings about this question.

Many, perhaps most, have no choice regarding their sexual attraction.[7] When a person is gay, bisexual, or transgender, they are faced with significant social and spiritual challenges. The same is true for those who have LGBTQ family members. Some LGBTQ individuals regularly hear hateful or hurtful comments from Church members—statements that they are deviant or a mistake. For these individuals, and particularly youth, the stigma of being gay can cause them to question their self-worth, which in some cases can result in depression or even thoughts of suicide. Some feel that Utah's high youth suicide rate is directly related to the Church's position.[8]

While sustaining our leaders, we must recognize how the Church's policies on LGBTQ matters can be for many, perhaps ourselves included, heavy and hurtful. Regardless of our own viewpoints, we can and should reach out with empathy, putting ourselves in others' shoes. For a parent whose gay son commits suicide or for the family member who knows their lesbian sister can never experience romantic love as a faithful member, we can see how they might struggle to trust the Church or its leaders or feel like they fit in or find meaning and relevance in our doctrines. For those members who are gay, the challenge is even greater, and many leave.

In the *Faith Crisis Member Survey,* one respondent wrote, "I am gay and don't feel emotionally safe at church." Another wrote:

> The reason I have stopped attending church is entirely because I am a lesbian. I am aware of all of the issues with various doctrines and church structures that people have, and I can cope with those. It would be nice if there was more transparency about some things, but I do not expect the Church to be perfect or have all the answers. All I want is to be accept[ed] for who I am and how Heavenly Father made me, and to not be excommunicated or labelled an apostate if I want to start a family with a same-sex spouse.

Kristine, who serves in a stake Relief Society presidency, has a twenty-five-year-old gay son. She shared that while attending a Relief Society meeting, a member who had just moved in from California introduced herself. She said that the reason she and her husband felt like they needed to sell their home and move was the tolerance and prevalence of gay people and gay marriage in their hometown. So, in this woman's words, they moved to get away from an environment they thought would "damage" their children and to be closer to God and with more faithful people. For this faithful stake leader who listened to this comment, and others like it, it can be complicated and difficult to be faithful while hoping that Church culture will one day welcome her son regardless of his sexual orientation. She struggles to make church a welcoming place for all who want to come unto Christ. Once, she walked out of sacrament meeting when the main speaker used the Family Proclamation to discuss the evils of the world and the calamities that God would cause to come to pass because of gay people and gay marriage. At times she feels that she is treated differently or rejected because she has a gay son. When that happens, the messages that she hears is that she is a failure and won't have any of the blessings promised as part of the gospel.

It can be difficult for someone who isn't gay or transgender to understand how the teachings of the Church impact a LGBTQ member's self-identity, outlook, and well-being. Caitlin Ryan studied the lives of LGBTQ youth and acceptance by their family, particularly in Latter-day Saint families. She said,

> As I learned more about the culture of the Mormon world and Mormon families, I realized that what I was seeing was a multi-dimensional level of rejection. It was the rejection by their family, the rejection by their church and their culture, and the rejection for eternity because they would lose their

family and all of these connections for eternity. . . . If you were a Mormon and you were gay, there was not a place for you.[9]

In a 2017 poll, 4.1 percent of Americans identified as LGBTQ.[10] If we assume the same rate of prevalence in the Church, that means that of the Church's approximately six million members in the United States, over 246,000 are LGBTQ; even if most of these people no longer attend, at least one gay, bisexual, trans or queer member is likely present in every congregation. President M. Russell Ballard has addressed the Church's need to reach out more to our gay brothers and sisters. He said,

> [Latter-day Saint] leaders, along with the rank and file, need to listen to and understand what LGBT[Q] members are feeling and experiencing. We must do better than we have in the past until all feel they have a spiritual home . . . a place to worship and serve the Lord.[11]

By listening to others, striving to understand their perspective, and validating their feelings, we build a bridge that shows we love and care regardless of our differences.

Unequal Gender Roles

In the *Faith Crisis Member Survey*, I asked, "How much do gender roles within the Church contribute to an individual's faith crisis?" Overall, 72 percent responded that it strongly contributes, with another 27 percent responding that it contributes. Women feel this more strongly, as 77 percent responding that it strongly contributes, while only 59 percent of men felt so. An astounding total of 99 percent of respondents believe that gender roles within the Church contribute to a faith crisis.

People's views regarding gender roles within the Church are diverse and take different forms. Referring to women in the Church, one woman wrote in a survey comment,

> Our experience is much like our mothers. We are told we are equal and powerful and relevant, except that we aren't. We hold no power, no real decision-making. We are presided over in every aspect of the gospel. It's suffocating and disempowering.

Some men and women have joined Ordain Women, an organization advocating for priesthood ordination for women. Some are more quiet about their belief in female priesthood ordination, while others don't advocate for priesthood ordination at all but still want to have more women in decision-making roles. Still others want greater cultural acceptance of the diverse ways women can choose to live their lives. When it comes to gender equality, there are many concerns.

Whole books have been written on the topic, including Neylan McBaine's *Women at Church: Magnifying LDS Women's Local Impact*. In the book's introduction, McBaine writes, "This book is predicated on a single belief: that there is much more we can do to see, hear, and include women at church."[12] She recognizes that many women "feel unseen, unheard, and unused," and calls for Latter-day Saints to have greater empathy and find ways to better involve and include women. In her book, McBaine relates a story about a conversation that Elder Ballard had with a stake Relief Society president:

> "Elder Ballard," she said, her voice edged with exasperation, "will the brethren in leadership positions ever understand that the sisters want to make a contribution to the real issues facing the Church and its members? . . . I feel like I'm the hired help at the council table. I'm there to serve, but not to contribute. When they talk about ways to accomplish the mission of the church, my opinion is never sought. And when they refer to the decisions of stake leaders, they never acknowledge me as a leader who can make a contribution to the spiritual growth and development of stake members. Sometimes they even talk about ways to meet the needs of the sisters in our stake without even inviting me to participate. I'm given assignments, and I do what I'm told. But I never feel that I am asked to counsel."[13]

This experience is likely familiar to many women leaders in the Church. The lack of women in decision-making positions in the Church is troublesome for many Latter-day Saints. One woman commented in the *Faith Crisis Member Survey*, "There are many decisions made that, had women been part of the process, I think the outcome would be very different. We see things from a different perspective, and our input is just as inspired and valuable."

Because of their different backgrounds, men and women see issues differently. If our leadership councils are largely male and if our speakers are mostly men, some members can feel (and sometimes rightly so) that Church leaders are not considering all points of view and are in danger of making some gendered mistakes. These mistakes are manifest in stories about a bishop who encouraged a woman to be silent about her husband's abuse because her husband had a promising career[14] or about a man who was told by his leader to "control your wife" when she chose to nurse in the Church foyer.[15]

We see gender inequality throughout the Church. We see it in large settings like general conferences, in which only one or two out of dozens of speakers in the general sessions are female, as well as in smaller, local settings, such as Primary sharing time, where almost all the stories told and songs sung are about boys. In stake council meetings, three female leaders usually attend, sitting alongside eighteen or more male leaders. Women rarely attend any bishopric or stake presidency meeting where critical issues and decisions are made. We use titles for men in leadership, including *President, Elder,* and *Bishop,* while special titles are rarely applied to women, even if they are in leadership roles. Because of the Proclamation on the Family and the importance the Church places on motherhood within the family, we often stress traditional gender roles for mothers and fathers, even though some men and women feel those roles are not right for them. Scripture is mostly written by men about men, and even though we have an expansive theology that includes a Mother in Heaven, we rarely mention her as a role model for our female members. In fact, we rarely mention her at all. Some refer to men as "the priesthood," and though only men are ordained to the priesthood in the Church, we know that women have priesthood authority through their temple covenants and through their callings within the Church.[16] (Specific ways we can address gender inequality are discussed in Chapter 10.)

While their limited involvement as equal partners in the Church may be a source of pain for many women, the most troubling aspect of gender disparity for others centers on the temple and polygamy. Amanda said she felt a "crushing anxiety" by the gender-specific language in the temple that implied that there was a man between her and her relationship with God. (Some of this language was removed or altered in January 2019.) She also described becoming physically ill when she read the Gospel Topic Essay on Joseph Smith's polygamy, learning about it for the first time. Even though polygamy is not practiced today, vestiges of it live on in the temple, in which a living man getting married for a second time can be sealed to his new wife even if he is still sealed to his first wife. A woman, on the other hand, seeking to be sealed to someone else after a divorce, cannot be sealed to another man without getting permission to cancel her first sealing. Polygamy is still part of our eternal theology and remains in our scriptural cannon. I've read many accounts of women (and some men) who struggle with polygamy and the role that it places women in. I read this story years ago and it still haunts me:

> Recently my highly orthodox mother and I had a conversation that I found devastating. [They talked about the celestial kingdom.] She replied with a sad smile, "Oh, sweetie, I won't be there."
>
> Confused, I asked, "You won't be in the celestial kingdom? You're the best woman I know! How can you say you won't be there?"
>
> "Well, I make sure that I commit little sins—nothing big—just little sins like lying and being judgmental and other things—just enough so I don't have to go to the highest level of the celestial kingdom. So I'll never have to worry about that polygamy stuff."
>
> "Does Dad know this?"
>
> "Yes. We've talked about it and he understands."
>
> "So—so you won't be with Dad in heaven?"
>
> Sadly, Mom shook her head and said, "I just try not to think of it too much."[17]

For some, the issues listed here are just the tip of the iceberg when it comes to gender inequality in the Church, and the scope of this book is not to do an in-depth analysis of gender roles. Rather the goal here is to illustrate how and why many feel deeply that women are not sufficiently valued as full participants in the Church. For those who see a gap between what we should be and our actual behavior, or for those who feel our doctrine and practices treat women as lesser than men, retaining belief in the Church can be a struggle. These issues affect their trust in their leaders or cause them to feel like they don't have a real place in the Church. They may conclude that the teachings and doctrines of the Church are not meaningful to them or even true.

Our theology, in its purest form, teaches that all, including women, are children of Heavenly Parents, with the potential to become like them. It is expansive and grand. It is ennobling and empowering, but often our sisters in the Church can feel like silent supporters, basking in the reflected glory of their husband, or worse, like second-class citizens or objects to be possessed and used.

Feelings of Judgment and Anxiety at Church

Jana Riess's recently published study included a survey of persons who have left the Church. According to her findings, 32 percent of women said that "if ward members had been more loving and less judgmental," they might have been induced to keep coming to church.[18] I'm sure this sentiment also applies to men, although perhaps to a lesser extent. In another study, Benjamin Knolls and Riess looked at Latter-day Saints, dividing them into "true believers" and those with doubt about the Church and its teachings. The survey found that 60.4 percent of doubters agreed with the statement "At the end of church, I usually feel tired or burned out," whereas only 11.4 percent of believers agreed with the statement.[19]

In my *Faith Crisis Member Survey*, I asked, "How much does feeling judged within the Church contribute to an individual's faith crisis?" Overall, 24 percent responded that it strongly contributes, with another 57 percent responding that it contributes. Although 81 percent of respondents believe judgment contributes to a faith crisis, it was maybe a secondary factor stemming from other issues such as their struggles with Church history, gender issues, and the Church's treatment of LGBTQ persons.

Even though we often sing "Where Can I Turn for Peace" in sacrament meeting, some do not feel peace; rather, they feel judged and experience high levels of anxiety while attending church. For example, for over a year Amanda attended church every week but became increasingly frustrated and anxious. She would notice things that she hadn't seen before, and she experienced what she called "debilitating anxiety." On Saturday morning she would wake up and feel terrible in anticipation of church the next day. Being an open and authentic person, it was difficult to be closeted about her beliefs, and she often felt like she was an imposter.

For some, the pain becomes so great that it becomes impossible to attend church meetings. Here are some comments from the *Faith Crisis Member Survey* of those who feel judgment or anxiety while at church:

> While standards are good, we have a culture dripping with perfectionism and works for salvation.

> Mormon culture has created a church of exclusion rather than inclusion.

> I do not believe in so much of the cultural judgment and policies that are used as hammers towards members who struggle with doctrine, personal challenges, or financial insolvency.

While recognizing that salvation and exaltation are gifts of grace that we can never merit, we also recognize that we must do our part to access the full effects of the Atonement in our lives. We make and keep sacred covenants and repent and make our lives right when we do wrong. This desire to live right can create a culture in which we may feel we are never enough and feel shame when we fall short. We may try to impose our standards and beliefs on others, even in our church meetings. This happens when we police opinions or shut down conversations that are contrary to our own way of believing. Here are several comments from the *Faith Crisis Member Focus Group* that illustrate this point:

I went to Sunday School several months ago. The topic was eternal marriage. I was not married in the temple, and my husband has not been active during our marriage. When the teacher asked, "What are the blessings of eternal marriage?" Someone said, "To know God." I raised my hand and asked if people really believed that those who weren't sealed didn't know God. The response was more harsh and demoralizing than I expected. My bishop responded to the entire class that to know God, you have to do what He does. I felt very hurt that even after asking a question to try and help my ward members see that not everyone in class has the same life situation that they responded by keeping me on the outside rather than trying to make room for me in the conversation. This experience changed my relationship with the Church and with my ward. I still attend but not as frequently, and I no longer feel that my activity and participation is always beneficial to my own well-being.

I have LGBT[Q] family members. I am a woman with no legitimate voice in the church nor do I have access to general Church leaders. The reaction in my local ward and stake is to shun and reject anyone with questions or doubts. Church is not a safe place for faith concerns or growth. My faith is actually damaged by church attendance. I find healing and faith through prayer and reading and speaking with trusted family members.

At church I feel constantly judged by others and the doctrines itself. I am not good enough is the message I get week after week. There is a tremendous culture of guilt and shame that has plagued me for years at church.

Yesterday I taught gospel doctrine about the prophet Hosea. . . . I wanted to focus at one point on God's love for us and how God forgives and keeps reaching after us, time and time again. I said I believe that God loves me, but I struggle to *feel* that love. I was hoping to make space for others struggling with this. Instead I got the chief traditional member in the room, who frequently makes sure authentic discussions get shut down, going into mini-lecture mode (very kindly) about "the list"—all the things we should be doing so we're worthy to feel God's love (pray, read the scriptures, etc.). She met her goal. No one dared say they struggle with anything after her comment.

I've been on both sides. There have been times when I have been part of the problem. Wanting so much to make sure things were done right, I shamed, put down, or expressed judgment when I should have just shown love and compassion. I have also felt the judgment that comes from expressing a nontraditional viewpoint. I remember when the topic in Sunday School was David and Bathsheba, and I pointed out how David's power as king enabled him to take what he wanted and that Bathsheba was unlikely able to refuse him, making this an instance of rape. Well, the class wanted nothing to do with that thought, and we returned to a discussion of avoiding pornography. That experience didn't damage my faith, but it added to my awareness of how some feel when we don't take the time to listen, even if their thoughts seem slightly different from our typical discussions.

Let's put ourselves in the shoes of those who are different and see how sometimes our meetings can be full of anxiety and implicit judgment. Maybe next Sunday, visualize how the entire Church experience would feel if you were:

- A closeted single gay man.
- A single woman who will likely never marry.
- Part of a couple who couldn't have children.
- A youth whose parents both work.
- A woman who sees much of the Old Testament as nonliteral stories.
- A young man who returned home early from his mission because of mental health.
- One of those who read, study, and pray and have only a hope that the gospel is true.
- A man who struggles with issues in Church history.
- Anyone who struggles with perfectionism in a church that stresses worthiness.

We are human—it's partly our nature to compare ourselves with others and notice our differences. Building bridges means learning about how someone else feels in our church community so that we can acknowledge, comfort, and accept those who are different than us.

Concern about Prophetic Leadership and Revelation

Some who are experiencing challenges to their faith often strive to find strong spiritual guidance. In the early Church, there were significant and dramatic spiritual events. Joseph Smith and others described heavenly visitations, dramatic outpourings of the Spirit, and the rapid unfolding of the Restoration. Joseph translated the Book of Mormon through divine inspiration, and he and others received revelations that we accept as scripture in the Doctrine and Covenants.

In our time, prophetic leadership is different and the revelatory way prophets and apostles lead the Church is more structured and less transparent. The Church is spread throughout the world in over thirty thousand congregations, a big difference from Joseph Smith's Kirtland, Missouri, or Nauvoo. The Church now has thousands of employees and the demands of a large organization operating in many diverse countries, each with complex legal and cultural differences. At times, the Church feels like a very large and almost business-like organization.

When members expect modern-day prophetic leadership to be accompanied by heavenly visitations, new scripture, and the establishment of new spiritual doctrines, they may become disappointed. Some may choose to look for spiritual outpourings with Latter-day Saint revivalists. Others begin to view the Church, with its large size, hierarchal structure, and policies, as just another opaque, bureaucratic, and corporatized organization. When the culture of even our local organizations begins to feel like a business, some feel that the Church can no longer provide answers to their spiritual questions or a community of worship.

Cultural and Language Issues

Church members frequently say that one of the best parts of the Church is that it is the same everywhere, and this statement is true when it comes to doctrine, ordinances, and structure. But each ward throughout the world has a unique culture. Wards and stakes are each a wonderful mixture of what inidividual members can bring to the table. These differences, however, can sometimes result in extra challenges for people who try to join one of these church communities but who are outside of that culture. For example, for foreign-born, non-native English speakers, feeling a sense of belonging in congregations in the United States can be especially difficult. Having lived in England, India, and Africa, I know that the Church can appear as an "American church" to many, and it is sometimes not sensitive to local customs that seem foreign to leaders from the United States. I did a study of my stake's membership records and compared the activity rate of converts who were born in the United States with the activity rate of those born outside of the United States. Not surprisingly, those born outside of the United States had substantially lower rates of activity. One intuitive conclusion is that those with a different native language or culture can sometimes feel like outsiders in the Church.

But culture extends beyond language and national origin. Some who support liberal politics struggle to reconcile their political and social beliefs with the overarching conservative culture within the Church in the

United States. Others feel they don't belong because they are introverted and feel uncomfortably exposed in a church that encourages sociality, public speaking, and extroverted behavior. For those who struggle financially, they may feel inferior in a culture where Church members often preach a prosperity gospel—one that inappropriately conflates righteousness with economic blessings and prosperity.

Political Conservatism

While the Church has a position of political neutrality and only rarely expresses an opinion on specific governmental actions,[20] Church members in the United States are predominantly Republican.[21] Because of this it is not uncommon for members to use key principles of the gospel to express support for specific political policies in church settings—almost all of which are politically conservative. I remember hearing that, when Elder Larry Echo Hawk was called as a seventy, some expressed concern because he was a Democrat who had served in President Barack Obama's administration.

In her research, Riess found "indications that those who disaffiliate may do so for reasons that are as political as they are theological. It's not that these young adults have abandoned belief in God, but that the church's conservatism on social issues has become an obstacle to their continued participation."[22] I suspect that many liberal millennials just don't find a home with us and leave.

Mental and Emotional Challenges

When a person suffers from mental illness or has significant emotional challenges, finding meaning and belonging at church may be difficult. Mental illness comes in different forms and probably affects all of us or our families in some way. The National Institute of Health estimates that "nearly one in five US adults lives with a mental illness."[23] The rate is higher among adolescents aged twelve to seventeen. Mental illness takes many forms, including major depression, PTSD, anxiety, bipolar disorders, obsessive-compulsive disorder, ADHD, eating disorders, and personality disorders. Someone who has never experienced mental illness may find it difficult to understand how debilitating it can be. The world just isn't the same, and church may be extra difficult. People may feel pressure to do everything that the Church and its culture requires of them when, at the same time, they can barely get out of bed in the morning.

On Sundays, we put on our best clothes, faces, and personalities when we attend church. We want to be and appear faithful. But mental illness is often hidden—people cannot see depression like they can a lost limb. Others may not be aware of a person's despair when they see them dressed in their best, handsome and beautiful, but lost on the inside. The talks and testimonies given at church often include stories of spiritual experiences in which people have found answers to complex health, economic, or emotional challenges. In these moments, we often express thanks for the miracles in our lives and how we have overcome our problems. But for a Church member with depression, anxiety, or another form of mental illness, their church experience will likely be substantially different. While the rest of us sing "On This Day of Joy and Gladness," they may feel that God doesn't love them because they don't have feelings of joy. A well-meaning conversation with another member, who shows love and interest by asking questions, may cause that person to feel overwhelmed because of anxiety. Some may feel unworthy because they can't seem to shake the darkness that haunts them and because they haven't experienced the miracle of having their burden taken away.

In her book *Silent Souls Weeping*, Jane Clayson Johnson describes her own episode of depression that came when she stopped feeling messages from the Spirit:

> For long stretches of time, I couldn't feel the Spirit. I did the right things: said my prayers, read my scriptures, and went to the temple, But, I didn't *feel* anything. It was as if the most important part of my soul had been carved out of me.[24]

For many, unable to feel the Spirit or any way to overcome their feelings of stigma and disconnection, they leave.

In 2013, Elder Jeffrey L. Holland gave a remarkable address on mental health challenges and spoke of the "dark night of the mind and spirit," stating, "I once terrifyingly saw it in myself."[25] Despite the compassion conveyed in his talk, Church members still sometimes subtly or inadvertently imply that mental illness is related to spiritual weakness. As a result, it's not surprising that for some, the doctrines of the Church are unable to pass through the barriers of emotional or mental pain and implant meaning in their hearts. When Church members judge worthiness based on what they can see, a person can feel that they are putting up a façade and that they don't truly belong.

Unique Millennial Issues

Chapter 2 highlighted how society is changing, with millennials having distinctively different values than previous generations. When looking at key beliefs such as the literal resurrection of Jesus Christ, the reality of God, life after death, and the Plan of Salvation, millennials are between 14 and 26 percent less certain about these beliefs.[26] They have higher concerns about some of the issues that I have already mentioned, including gender roles, LGBTQ inclusiveness, political conservatism, and mental and emotional challenges. And perhaps because of the general millennial mistrust of authority, they are less trusting of modern prophets and less certain of Joseph Smith's prophetic role.[27] Riess's *The Next Mormons: How Millennials Are Changing the LDS Church* gives a comprehensive view of these areas and should be required reading for anyone who wants to understand issues of faith for millennial Latter-day Saints.

Some Assumptions to Reconsider

In addition to understanding the above reasons that cause some Church members to struggle with their faith, we may need to question some commonly held assumptions about why people stop believing. For instance, it is not uncommon for someone to claim that a loss of faith can be prevented by simply reading scriptures, having sincere and searching prayers, and worshiping in the temple regularly. Contrary to this assumption, many who have found themselves in a crisis of faith say that they have never read the scriptures more, never prayed harder, and never worshiped in the temple more ardently than they did when they were unsuccessfully struggling to recover their former belief.

In the *Faith Crisis Member Survey*, I asked about individuals' religious practices at the time of their faith crisis.

- 86% believed wholeheartedly in the teachings of the Church.
- 98% held a temple recommend.
- 98% were keeping all the commandments.
- 64% were reading their scriptures daily.[28]
- 82% were having meaningful personal prayer.
- 99% attended church weekly.
- 79% of those who were endowed attended the temple regularly.

Some will perhaps say, "Well, they must not have been reading sincerely or ardently enough or long enough." Though I don't know what is in some people's hearts, I do know that if I am to build a bridge, I need to believe what those in faith crises say when they talk about their feelings; I need to accept the sincerity of their beliefs and the reality of their opinions. While I believe in the importance of scripture study, prayer, and temple worship, I realize that this is not a guaranteed plan to retain or regain a testimony.

Likewise, somewhere along the way, many of us have come to believe that people who stopped believing did so because they were offended, had conflict with leaders, or wanted to sin. Perhaps we used these reasons to remind ourselves of the importance of forgiveness, diligence, and obedience. In both the *Local Leader Survey* and the *Faith Crisis Member Survey*, I asked what factors contribute to an individual's faith crisis. Local leaders and members had vastly different responses:

What Factors Contribute to an Individual's Faith Crisis?

	Local Leader Survey		*Faith Crisis Member Survey*	
	Strongly Agree	Agree	Strongly Agree	Agree
Being offended	43.1%	47.4%	1.0%	18.0%
Conflict with other members	39.6%	53.9%	4.0%	54.0%
Not wanting to live the commandments	33.7%	50.6%	0.0%	9.0%

Clearly there is some disconnect between why people lose faith or leave the Church and why Church leaders *think* they do. In the *Faith Crisis Member Survey*, one commenter said,

> Change the narrative on why people leave. We often are not offended by the local people or want to sin. Many times, we are looking for any reason to stay. When people doubt or find legitimate, worrisome facts about the history or doctrinal practices, they need love and reassurance and a safe place to ask questions.

Unfortunately, church can be an unsafe place for those with questions or doubts, especially when we, their fellow Church members, are judgmental of their feelings. We may, for instance, look down on them for not aligning with our own personal standards—for things such as watching R-rated movies, drinking caffeinated beverages, or not observing the Sabbath like we think they should. Although we may think we can clearly see how what someone is or isn't doing is affecting their faith, the reality is more complicated. Often, we only understand what we can see from the outside; rarely can we see the whole person, including what is inside their heart. When we cast blame on those losing their faith, doubt their sincerity, or offer cliché solutions to their concerns, they will lose confidence in their relationships with us and we will lose the trust that comes when we treat their experiences and feelings as real.

It is worth mentioning that offering advice to those who we think are choosing to be offended or who are facing faith challenges rarely works and frequently backfires. According to scientific research, "whenever someone tells us what to do and how to do it, we respond with a defensive *defiance* because we want to maximize our personal freedom and decision making."[29] The referenced research goes on to conclude, "If we *really* want to encourage behavior (or belief) change in others we actually need to move away from advice giving (especially when our advice is unsolicited) and toward *modeling*. In other words, we need to be an *example* for others rather than telling them what to do."[30] The behavior that is most effective in ministering is loving, listening, and trying to understand without judgment. This is what bridge building is all about—finding common ground and building a firm and constant foundation.

Some of the factors discussed in this chapter are ones you may have already deeply thought about, and there may be some other factors that I have omitted—such as unfulfilled promises of marriage, children, wealth, or health. Every person is different, and thus each person's reasons for struggling with or losing their faith will slightly differ. Some of the issues overlap, and some people struggle with several of them all at once. Even though it may be hard to think about all of these difficult issues, understanding what those struggling with faith are facing is part of the ground upon which our bridge of empathy and love must be set, and we must therefore find a way to face it. Upon that ground it is crucial that we choose the correct materials and tools—that is, the approaches and strategies—for our bridge to stand firm.

CHAPTER 4

Confronting Today's Challenges of Faith

For those of you who earnestly seek to bear another's burdens, it is important that you refortify yourself and build yourself back up when others expect so much of you and indeed take so much out of you. No one is so strong that he or she does not ever feel fatigued or frustrated or recognize the need to care for themselves. Jesus certainly experienced that fatigue, felt the drain on His strength. He gave and gave, but there was a cost attached to that, and He felt the effects of so many relying on Him. When the woman with an issue of blood touched Him in the crowd, He healed her, but He also noted that "virtue had gone out of him."

—Elder Jeffrey R. Holland[1]

Avoiding difficult subjects is no longer an option for those who wish to build and maintain bridges with those going through a crisis of faith. While reading the scriptures, praying, and keeping the commandments are certainly helpful, if not essential, for building and maintaining testimonies, they cannot guarantee that someone would not face a challenge to or lose their faith in the Restoration. Many have lost faith despite doing all these things, and I respect that their study was diligent, that their prayers were sincere, and that they didn't have some secret sin preventing them from having the Spirit. If they had lived in an earlier time and had never been exposed to modern challenges, both inside and outside the Church, perhaps their faith wouldn't have changed at all.

By familiarizing ourselves with challenges to faith and learning strategies to best address them, we will be better able to confidently and sincerely minister to our own. Our faith and the faith we teach our children and those we serve needs to take into consideration and address what they might be facing. This chapter focuses on principles that are useful in helping faith grow. They have helped my testimony grow richer and deeper and have given me insights into how to minister with more compassion, empathy, and understanding.

Study Church History

Ministering to those with questions and doubts requires that we understand the issues that are challenging them. In recent years, the Church has made great efforts to provide better information on its history through sources such as the Gospel Topics Essays, the Joseph Smith Papers, and its recently published history, *Saints: The Story of the Church of Jesus Christ in the Latter Days.*[2]

The Gospel Topics Essays were commissioned by Church leaders to address subjects relating to our history that could be difficult for some members—especially when first encountering them from sources antagonistic to the Church. According to President M. Russell Ballard, they "provide balanced and reliable interpretations of the facts for controversial and unfamiliar Church-related subjects,"[3] including polygamy, the translation of the Book of Mormon and Book of Abraham, race and the priesthood, the Mountain Meadows Massacre, and more.[4] Getting to know these topics is crucial for understanding our brothers and sisters whose faith might be challenged by these complexities.

If a ministering sister has never heard about seer stones, how does she build an authentic relationship with a woman who is troubled by the use of seer stones in the Book of Mormon translation? When a bishop doesn't know about the differing accounts of the First Vision, how can he help a young couple that is considering leaving the Church because they just found out about them? If a parent wants to prepare her daughter to serve a mission, should she not have a better understanding of the beginnings of the Church's past practice of polygamy before her contacts and investigators ask her questions about it?

All of these are a part of our history—we need to own, understand, and incorporate their implications into our own faith and ministry. Latter-day Saint historian and scholar Patrick Mason, author of *Planted: Belief and Belonging in an Age of Doubt*, says the following about the importance of better understanding the relationship of faith and Church history:

> The Gospel Topics Essays and the new *Saints* history, with its accompanying online support materials, are terrific resources. It seems clear to me that the Church leadership wants every member to become familiar with Church history, including some of the more difficult issues, by availing themselves of these resources. But the essays and the book only do half of the work. Getting the history right is essential, but readers are left to make meaning out of the historical facts that are presented to them. History never interprets itself. Therefore, each member has to do the hard work of determining what this history means for them, and how they incorporate it into their testimony of the restoration of the gospel of Jesus Christ.[5]

We don't need to get PhDs or become experts on Church history. We can read at our own pace and decide what level of detail we need to know to be effective parents, leaders, and ministers. But one way or another, we must better understand our history and where we as Latter-day Saints came from. As members and local leaders, we need to take the initiative to learn about our complex history and be willing to discuss it in those places where we have responsibility—in our families and in our wards.

President M. Russell Ballard, as a member of the Quorum of the Twelve Apostles, gave a landmark address called "Opportunities and Responsibilities of CES Teachers in the 21st Century" to the Church's religious educators in February 2016. In what ought to be required reading for understanding how we should address historical and doctrinal issues, President Ballard spoke on the imperative to first better inform ourselves of our history:

> Gone are the days when a student asked an honest question and a teacher responded, "Don't worry about it!" Gone are the days when a student raised a sincere concern and a teacher bore his or her testimony as a response intended to avoid the issue. Gone are the days when students were protected from people who attacked the Church.
>
> It was only a generation ago that our young people's access to information about our history, doctrine, and practices was basically limited to materials printed by the Church. Few students came in contact with alternative interpretations. Mostly, our young people lived a sheltered life. Our curriculum at that time, though well-meaning, did not prepare students for today—a day when students have instant access to virtually everything about the Church from every possible point of view.
>
> You should be among the first, outside your students' families, to introduce authoritative sources on topics that may be less well-known or controversial, so your students will measure whatever they hear or read later against what you have already taught them.
>
> Church leaders today are fully conscious of the unlimited access to information, and we are making extraordinary efforts to provide accurate context and understanding of the teachings of the Restoration. A prime example of this effort is the 11 Gospel Topics essays on LDS.org that provide balanced and reliable interpretations of the facts for controversial and unfamiliar Church-related subjects. It is important that you know the content in these essays like you know the back of your hand.[6]

According to President Ballard, because of the internet and increased availability of information, teachers—particularly parents and teachers of youth—should be better prepared to assist those who come to them for help on these matters.

Unfortunately, I have heard Church members and even some leaders discourage others from reading the essays, fearing that they might unnecessarily have their faith challenged by them. Shielding people from this information, however, is not a sustainable solution. As Elder Steven R. Snow, emeritus Church Historian and Recorder, has said, "My view is that being open about our history solves a whole lot more problems than it creates. We might not have all the answers, but if we are open (and we now have pretty remarkable transparency), then I think in the long run that will serve us well."[7]

Some may wonder: If I study these issues, will I risk losing my faith? If I teach these issues, will I risk hurting others' faith? The honest answer is: Yes. Faith can always be challenged, but becoming more literate in our history doesn't need to threaten our faith. To the contrary, it can and ought to strengthen our faith and help us understand God's work in the Church and in the word. On this, Patrick Mason says:

> Each of us now has to decide what to do with that information. For some people, such information has and will carry them out of the Church, as it destroys a more pristine image they had in mind of the Church, its leaders, and its history. But it doesn't have to. It seems that the fundamental question we have to ask about the history is, "What does this tell me about the way that God works in the world? How does this help me better understand what it means for Christ to redeem everything—not just our souls, but our history, our church, our leaders, our society?" We're not going to make progress by going around, under, or over the history. We have to go straight through it. That's what Christ did in Gethsemane—he went straight through the best and worst of the human condition, not around it. If we want to participate with him in the ongoing restoration of the gospel and redemption of the world, we have to do the same.[8]

It's our responsibility to develop and mature our testimonies and faith. At times, the work is hard, but in the process, we will learn and develop empathy and compassion. I used to think faith was supposed to be easy— I was wrong. Faith is a lifelong pursuit and involves incorporating new life experiences into our belief without being sheltered from the complexities of history, culture, humanness, uncertainty, and all that life brings us. I have found the journey challenging but rich, and I don't wish to go back to those days when it all seemed simple.

Focus on the Savior Jesus Christ

The Church was restored to help us come unto Jesus Christ. Only in and through our Savior can we receive the blessings of the Atonement and return to live with our Heavenly Parents. We should build our faith on Jesus Christ and focus our lives on the doctrine of Christ and the beauty and grace of the Plan of Salvation, made available through His Atonement. We should always keep Christ as our focus, especially when we encounter and discuss challenges.

This focus on Christ is a constant in all we believe, and we should hear it in everything we do. Church leaders are taught, "Priesthood and auxiliary leaders and teachers strive to help others become true followers of Jesus Christ."[9] Missionaries are instructed to "invite others to come unto Christ by helping them receive the restored gospel." [10] Parents are counseled, "Parents fulfill [their] responsibility by teaching their children to follow Jesus Christ and live His gospel."[11] Jacob in the Book of Mormon sums it up when he says,

> We labor diligently to write to persuade our children, and also our brethren, to believe in Christ. . . . And we talk of Christ, we rejoice in Christ, we preach of Christ, we prophesy of Christ, and we write according to our prophecies, that our children may know to what source they may look for a remission of their sins. (2 Ne. 25:23, 26)

There is no other way.

When I was a mission president, our missionaries and I would regularly study the Christlike attributes identified in *Preach My Gospel*.[12] Let's review a few of them to see how they can help build and strengthen faith through today's challenges:

- *Faith in Jesus Christ*. The Atonement is referred to as infinite. I have confidence this means that if we come unto Him, all will be made right. I can be confident in the gospel plan and His cornerstone role. I also believe that through His Atonement, He knows us completely, having taken upon Him our pains, sicknesses, and infirmities, and He knows how to succor us (see Alma 7:11). I can confidently say, "Lord, I believe; help thou mine unbelief" (Mark 9:24).

- *Hope*. According to *Preach My Gospel*, "Hope is an abiding trust that the Lord will fulfill His promises to you."[13] Accepting the perfect love of Him and our Heavenly Parents gives us confidence that He won't let us down. That hope helps get us through times when we don't have faith and helps us when challenges—even the challenges we have discussed here—seem overwhelming. We can have confidence in the future, although that future may be distant. He keeps His promises.

- *Charity and Love.* Charity and love are key principles for ministering to those who question. They are also principles that apply to the imperfect people around us. This attribute requires restraint: "You will avoid judging others, criticizing them, or saying negative things about them. You will try to understand them and their points of view. You will be patient with them and try to help them when they are struggling or discouraged."[14]

- *Patience.* Submitting to the Lord's timeline, accepting that all will not be right until the end, and having confidence in the ultimate goodness of other people are the Savior's way. "You must be patient with all people, yourself included."[15]

Christ's ministry goes far beyond modeling perfecting characteristics. His ministry includes story after story of him healing others. He healed the blind man at the pool of Bethesda (John 5:5–9), the crippled woman (Luke 13:11–13), and the ten with leprosy (Luke 17:11–14). He even raised the dead (Mathew 9:23–25, Luke 7:11–15, John 11:38–44). He did this not only to relieve suffering but also to teach us that through Him, we can be healed. By highlighting these stories of healing, we can teach that healing is offered universally to all who are broken, diseased, or unclean.

We can also highlight the universal nature of Christ's teachings and His gospel. Several times in His life, He taught us that His message is for every one of our Heavenly Parents children. He reached out to the women with an issue of blood (Mark 5:25–34). The story of the Good Samaritan highlights our responsibility to serve and bless others' lives (Luke 10:25–37). Christ's teaching of the adulterous Samaritan woman at the well illustrates his love to people who commit sin or are different than us (John 4:1–26). In modern scripture the Lord tells us of the universal nature of His message. He says, "For, verily, the sound must go forth from this place into all the world, and unto the uttermost parts of the earth—the gospel must be preached unto every creature" (D&C 58:64).

Alma teaches about the depth of Christ's Atonement when he says,

And he shall go forth, suffering pains and afflictions and temptations of every kind; and this that the word might be fulfilled which saith he will take upon him the pains and the sicknesses of his people. And he will take upon him death, that he may loose the bands of death which bind his people; and he will take upon him their infirmities, that his bowels may be filled with mercy, according to the flesh, that he may know according to the flesh how to succor his people according to their infirmities. (Alma 7:11–12)

The message of Christ is universal; it is one of healing; it is one of complete understanding. And because He knows us completely, we are never alone.

Church programs and leaders are not an end unto themselves. They are meant to help us come unto Christ by teaching and enabling us to love and serve others as he did. Our regard of and confidence in our leaders, past and present, and the institution of the Church are not the destination. They are the means whereby discipleship and our journey to be healed and become more Christlike begins.

Remember That People—Including Church Leaders—Make Mistakes

We can sustain, respect, and even revere our leaders while at the same time acknowledging that they are human and make mistakes. From our limited perspective, we may not know whether the mistakes made by our leaders are big or little or whether they affect a few people in a small way or more people in a significant way. We may not even know if something we find challenging is really a mistake at all or simply something we do not yet understand. Members of the Church do not always agree on whether or not something that happened in the past was a mistake. For example, there are faithful members who believe that Brigham Young was misguided when enacting a policy that denied priesthood and temple blessings to those of African descent. There are also members who believe the ban stemmed from divine revelation. Because of this, over the years some members and Church leaders speculated on why God would do such a thing, and sometimes even went as far as pointing to the restriction as evidence of white superiority. For this reason, the Church in 2013 issued a statement declaring, "None of these explanations is accepted today as the official doctrine of the Church," and that

> the Church disavows the theories advanced in the past that black skin is a sign of divine disfavor or curse, or that it reflects unrighteous actions in a premortal life; that mixed-race marriages are a sin; or that blacks or people of any other race or ethnicity are inferior in any way to anyone else. Church leaders today unequivocally condemn all racism, past and present, in any form.[16]

Remembering that our leaders are just like us and make mistakes can help give us patience when dealing with challenging issues. There is no temple recommend question that asks if we believe our leaders are infallible. We simply recognize their unique prophetic role in leading the Church of Jesus Christ and our willingness to sustain them. As we sustain them, we can be aware of the tremendous load they carry and pray for them, knowing that they are fully aware of their own personal limitations. We can have strong faith in Jesus Christ and the doctrines of the restored gospel even while believing that there have been mistakes in our past.

In their book *The Crucible of Doubt: Reflections On the Quest for Faith*, Latter-day Saint authors Fiona and Terryl Givens share a quote from Elder B. H. Roberts on the imperfection of Church leaders despite their efforts to be inspired in all things. He said,

> I think it is a reasonable conclusion to say that constant, never-varying inspiration is not a factor in the administration of the affairs even of the Church; not even good men, no not though they be prophets or other high officials of the Church, are at all times and in all things inspired of God.[17]

According to the Givenses, we can accept the weaknesses of our leadership while still sustaining them in their callings. They write,

> Airbrushing our leaders, past or present, is both a wrenching of the scriptural record and a form of idolatry. It generates an inaccurate paradigm that creates false expectations and disappointment. God specifically said that he called weak vessels so we wouldn't place our faith in their strength or power, but in God's. The prophetic mantle represents priesthood keys, not a level of holiness or infallibility. That is why our scripturally mandated duty to the prophets and apostles is not to idolize them but to uphold and sustain them "by the prayer of faith" (D&C 21:6).[18]

On April 6, 1830, the day the Church was first organized, the Prophet Joseph Smith received a revelation about his role. To the members, the Lord said, "For his word ye shall receive, as if from mine own mouth, in all patience and faith" (D&C 21:5). In patience and faith, we can sustain prophets and listen intently, being aware that they are humans, as we are, with spiritual experiences, a life devoted to building the kingdom, a focus on living a life pleasing to God, and authority to lead in their callings.

Examine What Is in Your Truth Cart

We all have things we once believed as true but no longer accept. As children many of us believed that every Christmas Eve a man in a red suit traveled across the globe with the aid of flying reindeer to deliver toys to every good child on the planet. Eventually we all learned that this wasn't the case—some of us more traumatized by the discovery than others—and were able to move on and still celebrate Christmas with joy. Similarly, most of us have some religious beliefs that we no longer hold true. For those of us who attended Primary as children, our faith was often simple and absolute. We completely trusted parents, teachers, and other authorities, and with our simple faith, we knew. As we grew older, the world became more complex and many of us encountered challenges to our faith. For many of us, our faith continues to change well into adulthood.

Some of my greatest spiritual growth has occurred long after my formative years as a young adult. That growth has come through patience, pondering, worship, and study. As a young adult, I thought I knew all the answers, but now I know that I didn't even know all the questions. Some of the things that I knew then, I still believe, and some I have completely discarded. For example, many of us perhaps once believed (or still believe) that the Earth was created 6,000 to 13,000 years ago, that Noah's Flood covered every inch of the planet, or that the Book of Mormon documented the sole ancestors of every indigenous person on both American continents. For some, new discoveries and scientific consensus have led them to no longer believe those teachings as they once did and to understand them in new light—perhaps offering a new appreciation for the Creation we experience around us and lessons on the need to follow Christ and God's prophets. Even if we no longer accept some things as literally true or in the same way as we once believed, we are able to view them in light of what we still believe.

Patrick Mason, at a conference of Latter-day Saint scholars seeking to defend the faith, introduced the concept of a "truth cart." A truth cart contains everything we believe is true, and sometimes it has things in it that aren't important in our mortal journey. He says,

> One of the problems we have in [Latter-day Saint culture] is that we have loaded too much into the Truth Cart. And then when anything in the cart starts to rot a bit, or look unseemly upon further inspection, some have a tendency to overturn the entire cart or seek a refund for the whole lot. We have loaded so much into the Truth Cart largely because we have wanted to have the same kind of certainty about our religious claims—down to rather obscure doctrinal issues—as we do about scientific claims. Over the years the church leadership and laity have also done our religion no favors by putting more in the cart than the cart could possible bear. . . . Many of the things which trouble people are things that we probably should never have been all that dogmatic about in the first place. I find that a little humility about our doctrine, especially given the contingencies of its historical development, goes a long way in remaining satisfied with the whole.[19]

At some point in our lives, the items we have placed in our truth cart may be challenged. In my truth cart, I hold my belief in our Heavenly Parents. I believe they are real, that we are their children, and that they love us in a perfect way. I believe they have done and will do everything that is possible to help us return to them. Their plan, which hinges on our Savior Jesus Christ, provides a perfect and expansive way for each of us to find eternal joy and wholeness. I have similar feelings about the Savior's Atonement and the Plan of Salvation, and our expansive doctrine applies to all of Heavenly Parents' children, regardless of time or location. I am grateful for the Restoration of the gospel and Joseph Smith's role in bringing these doctrines to the world. At the center of the Plan of Salvation is the eternal nature of family and relationships. I try to do my part in building and strengthening these relationships.

But there are other beliefs that, because of time and experience, I no longer hold. As already mentioned, as our understanding of the gospel and the world has expanded, we all have beliefs from our childhood, early years, and even late adulthood that we no longer claim. We are often okay with changing these beliefs and frequently do not realize until later that they have changed, partly because those beliefs didn't really matter in any practical way to our belief in the Savior, covenant keeping, or worthiness to enter into the temple. Personally, my list of doctrinal beliefs is not as long as it used to be, but my foundation is simpler, more durable, and more meaningful. The doctrine of Christ (see 2 Ne. 31; 3 Ne. 11:31–35; and 3 Ne. 27) is simple and summarized in the injunction to "come unto Christ by having faith in Jesus Christ and His Atonement" and to believe in "repentance, baptism, receiving the gift of the Holy Ghost, and enduring to the end."[20]

In our efforts to better understand our history or why loved ones no longer believe, we may encounter issues that challenge items in our truth cart. When that happens, we should decide if the item is an essential belief and whether it needs to be defended. If so, we should work to better understand it and do the work to incorporate the newfound issue into our core beliefs. If it isn't a core belief, we can let it go, toss it out of the cart, and not worry about it.

When I grew up, I believed that all Native Americans were descendants of Lehi and his family who came to the Americas from Jerusalem. The Church's introduction to the Book of Mormon, until recently, suggested as much.[21] In recent years, however, DNA studies have shown that indigenous populations in the Americas do not appear to be genetically related to the peoples of the Middle East.[22] While these studies have helped change some of my views about the Book of Mormon and its relationship to indigenous peoples, my core beliefs of the gospel are not affected. If prophets and other Church leaders were wrong about this in the past, it does not mean that they are no longer able to help me come unto Christ or have authority to administer saving ordinances and covenants.

Church leaders have even given us permission to have private disagreements about Church doctrines, practices, and principles. For example, Elder D. Todd Christofferson was asked in an interview whether Church members could support same-sex marriage while the Church was actively opposing it. He responded,

> We have individual members in the church with a variety of different opinions, beliefs and positions on these issues [same sex marriage] and other issues. In our view, it doesn't really become a problem unless someone is out attacking the church and its leaders—if that's a deliberate and persistent effort and trying to get others to follow them, trying to draw others away, trying to pull people, if you will, out of the Church or away from its teaching and doctrines.[23]

We each have to manage our truth carts, and one person's truth cart will likely be different than another's. But part of being an effective minister is recognizing and accepting that others will manage their truth carts differently. As we try to help people come unto Christ, we don't need to force them to believe precisely as you and me. The gospel of Jesus Christ is inclusive enough for a wide spectrum of different beliefs on things such as the age of the Earth, the ancestry of indigenous peoples, the reasons for the priesthood and temple restriction, or the details of polygamy. These issues, and many others, won't bring salvation or even earthly happiness. We can instead build a ministerial bridge on doctrines and beliefs that we share. For some, those beliefs might not even include God, the Savior, or prophetic callings. But for all but a very small group, they can entail living a good life with love, respect, and service to others. That's plenty of common ground on which we can build a trusting relationship.

Remember What You Do Know and Believe

If we question one belief, it doesn't mean that we have to question all the beliefs in our truth cart. In these moments of doubts, we should anchor ourselves to those beliefs we do hold. On this, Elder Jeffrey R Holland says,

> When problems come and questions arise, do not start your quest for faith by saying how much you do not have, leading as it were with your "unbelief." That is like trying to stuff a turkey through the beak! Let me be clear on this point: I am not asking you to pretend to faith you do not have. I am asking you to be true to the faith you do have. . . . Hope on. Journey on. Honestly

acknowledge your questions and your concerns, but first and forever fan the flame of your faith, because all things are possible to them that believe.[24]

When I get caught up in an issue, I reach into my memory for those times that I felt God's awareness and love for me. I hope we all have such experiences that form a basis of our belief that we can turn to for comfort and peace. When dealing with challenges to our faith, sometimes we may need moments of respite. In a General Conference talk addressing these moments, Elder Neal A. Andersen urges us to turn to those truths that we do hold: "At times, the Lord's answer will be 'You don't know everything, but you know enough'—enough to keep the commandments and to do what is right."[25] Part of being patient is knowing when to step back from examining faith-challenging issues and not letting our questions turn ourselves into skeptics. In their book *Faith Is Not Blind*, Elder Bruce C. Hafen and his wife Marie caution us to avoid overcorrecting in the opposite direction when we come upon something that challenges our faith: "We need to look longer and harder at difficult questions and pat answers, but without lurching from extreme innocence to extreme skepticism."[26] There is so much we don't know, but we do know or believe some things, and in most cases we might be surprised to discover that those few things are all we really need.

Sometimes we forget that even Joseph Smith had questions and doubts. Some of the darkest days for Joseph were while he was imprisoned in Liberty Jail. In March 1839 he wrote a letter to the Saints that later became Doctrine and Covenants 121. His loneliness and feelings of abandonment are expressed in his cry, "O God, where art thou? And where is the pavilion that covereth thy hiding place?" (v. 1). In response, the Lord tells him, "My son, peace be unto your soul; thine adversity and thine afflictions shall be but for a small moment" (v. 7). The Lord then outlines the characteristics required for a person to have priesthood power and influence, including long-suffering, gentleness, meekness, kindness, and an increase of love. We often think about these traits when considering how we should treat others, but we should treat ourselves the same way. We can remember what we know, be kind to our unbelief, and show ourselves a portion of God's love.

Expect That Your Faith Will Change and Continue to Grow

President Howard W. Hunter said, "The path [of finding God] is one that leads upward; it takes faith and effort and is not the easy course."[27]

My faith hasn't been an easy course and remains full of effort. Here are some questions that have helped me as I have grappled with various concerns related to my own faith:

- Is answering this question essential for my gospel understanding?

- If a mistake was made by a general or local Church leader, can I still believe in Heavenly Parents, an Atonement, and the Plan of Salvation?

- How should my faith change with what I now know?

- How can I ask a question with faith instead of with skepticism?

Each of us is unique and faces different challenges. Our faith will change and hopefully mature as we face these challenges and try to understand and feel empathy toward those around us. Whether our challenges are related to mental health, gender, race, sexual orientation, economics, age, or simply different ways of thinking, I have come to respect how individual our challenges are. We should never stop trying to better understand the challenges others carry. In that process, we change for the better and can better show love.

Be Comfortable with Not Having All the Answers

The reality is that not all questions will be answered and not all challenges will be taken from us in this life. One of the most helpful, albeit difficult, things we can do is learn how to live with this uncertainty and ambiguity. Terryl Givens offers the following on finding comfort in that which we do believe:

> I think in virtually every life there are grey areas, areas of uncertainty, which I think we should think more comfortable expressing as a way of indicating that, yes, even though I know this, I'm convicted of this particular truth, but I am still struggling and wrestling with these other areas of our faith tradition. I think that movement in that direction would eliminate the kind of silent trauma and sense of alienation that I think vast multitudes in our faith tradition experience as they sit quietly in their pews listening to these professions of certitude and knowledge and feeling that they are not a part of that tradition because they can't engage in that same kind of language when the reality is that they are probably in the majority in many cases. It is incumbent upon us to shape the culture that characterizes Mormonism.[28]

When we come to a complex or challenging issue, it's okay to not have the answer. We should not, however, confuse that with having no answers or belief. Elder Dieter F. Uchtdorf said,

> It's natural to have questions—the acorn of honest inquiry has often sprouted and matured into a great oak of understanding. There are few members of the Church who, at one time or another, have not wrestled with serious or sensitive questions. One of the purposes of the Church is to nurture and cultivate the seed of faith—even in the sometimes sandy soil of doubt and uncertainty. Faith is to hope for things which are not seen but which are true.[29]

Similarly, the *True to the Faith* manual reminds us: "Having faith in Him means relying completely on Him—trusting in His infinite power, intelligence, and love. It means believing that even though we do not understand all things, He does."[30]

This chapter doesn't answer all questions. For example, how does a person trust a Church leader after they feel the leader has made an egregious mistake? Or how does one keep trust in God after they feel He has not answered their prayers? How do you live in the ambiguity? For these questions, I have found answers—or at least peace. But my answers and peace aren't intellectual; they are the result of pondering, prayer, and life experience, and they may be different for someone else because we are all different and because God expects us to find our own way through. The principles I have described are guideposts which have been helpful in my journey. I pray they will be in yours.

Faith is a living thing. Even if we are never exposed to issues that challenge our faith, we should focus on continually building our faith. Just like our muscles, if we do not continually work to build and strengthen our faith, it will shrivel and become less meaningful and relevant to our lives. By confronting faith challenges using the strategies listed above, we are better prepared to love and minister to those facing their own faith challenges. And as we work with people who are losing their belief, we can use those moments as opportunities to both build a bridge of understanding and to grow our own faith.

CHAPTER 5

How Faith Changes

Choosing to increase our faith in the Savior isn't easy. It takes work, but the feelings inside of peace and joy and love are worth all our efforts.
—Patricia P. Pinegar [1]

My Faith Has Changed

When I finished my first mission, I had developed a testimony of Jesus Christ and the Atonement. I believed in the Plan of Salvation and was grateful for what it taught me about my identity as a child of God and how I wanted to live my life. Since then, I have had forty years to witness change around me and to grow. I have had disappointments and successes. There were periods when my faith remained vibrant, and I felt God's constant companionship. At other times my faith stagnated, and the heavens seemed closed. At other times I received a near constant stream of new thoughts and insights, giving me a deeper and richer appreciation of God's role in my life and his love for all his children. Through it all, I gained a greater awareness of the Savior's Atonement freeing me from not only the effects of sin but also the weakness and sickness within me, and I have felt the Savior's call: "Repent of your sins, and be converted that I may heal you" (3 Ne. 9:13). My appreciation for the Savior's ministry—his healing of the sick and possessed—has made my faith more personal and richer. Through the Atonement, all unfairness such as our birth culture, genetics, and other factors is removed; all is made right. I have more awareness of the challenges of the world but also hope and confidence in the love and plan of our Heavenly Parents.

Faith in Church Members and Leaders

As my faith has grown, it has also changed. For example, in a way it didn't before, my faith now acknowledges the limitations and mistakes of both Church members and Church leaders. And even though I have seen Latter-day Saints do things, sometimes in the name of the Lord, that were wrong and hurtful, I have developed compassion for the Church's leaders and my fellow members who try their best to accomplish the Lord's work. For the most part, these are good, albeit flawed, women and men who just want to help others in the best way they can.

Earlier in my life, I looked at Church leaders in such a reverential way that I couldn't conceive of them making mistakes. In our culture we often put Church leaders on a pedestal, and when they make mistakes or do or say something we don't agree with, it's easy to dismiss them as leaders altogether, assuming that if they were really inspired by God, they wouldn't have made a mistake. We know no one is perfect, yet it can still be tempting to demand perfection from our leaders. Perhaps we have this tendency because our leaders have a large influence over the Church, and we have high expectations of them because we want to feel God's direction in our lives. But we cannot demand from them what conditions of mortality do not allow. Instead, when we perceive that a Church leader or even a fellow member has made a mistake, we should work on cultivating the Christlike attributes of charity, kindness, and forgiveness. Elder Jeffrey R. Holland once gave a beautiful injunction:

> Be kind regarding human frailty—your own as well as that of those who serve with you in a church led by volunteer, mortal men and women. Except in the case of His only perfect Begotten Son, imperfect people are all God has ever had to work with. That must be terribly frustrating to Him, but He deals with it. So should we. And when you see imperfection, remember that the limitation is not in the divinity of the work. As one gifted writer has suggested, when the infinite fulness is poured forth, it is not the oil's fault if there is some loss because finite vessels can't quite contain it all. Those finite vessels include you and me, so be patient and kind and forgiving.[2]

This compassionate acknowledgment that we are all imperfect and make mistakes gives me hope that the mistakes that I have made in my family or when I was a Church leader will be in some way made right through the Atonement of Christ. Even with that awareness, however, there are times when I wake up in the dark morning feeling deep regret for specific instances where I fell short, mostly because of inexperience, knowing that on my own I cannot remove the burden that I added to others. All I can do is try and forgive myself and help others who have burdens.

Acceptance of leaders' mistakes is helpful for some. But for others, the actions of leaders may be devastating and have lifelong impact. I recall how my wife was assigned to work with a wonderful, beautiful woman who had been sexually assaulted by a Church leader as a teen. It had taken her years before she could be in a room alone with a man without feeling the trauma of that assault. I saw a glimpse of the healing power of the Atonement when, almost forty years after the assault, she let me lay my hands on her head and give her a blessing. Her healing won't be complete until the next life, but in that moment I witnessed the Lord's love and healing potential against the backdrop of a leader's wickedness. We can never know how the weaknesses and imperfections of a leader can affect another person. Our responsibility is to love and minister in their pain and suffering. The rest is up to the Savior to make right.

Accepting the humanness of Church leaders is just one way in which my faith has changed, and I am better because of it. I am more compassionate with others and with myself. I have more hope that even I, with all my limitations, can be healed of my prejudice, inexperience, weakness, and impatience.

God's Compassion in the Midst of Suffering

I want to share an example of another way in which my faith has changed. My wife and I lived in India for a year, leading a charity that focused on helping those affected with leprosy—some of the poorest and most marginalized people in the world. Following that, we served a mission in Sierra Leone, one of the poorest countries in Africa, that was cut short by the Ebola epidemic that killed more than ten thousand of God's children. In both areas, we saw people who had very difficult lives. Many didn't have tomorrow's food today; instead they lived hand to mouth in a way I only academically understand. I believe our Heavenly Parents love all their children, so how could so many of their children live such difficult lives?

Some have lost their belief in God while pondering these kinds of questions. After all, why would a loving God allow so many of his children to suffer without intervening? During this time, while being surrounded and overwhelmed by near universal suffering, I gained a greater awareness of the expansive view of the Atonement—that through it all will be made right. When the Savior made the world, we knew that it would become fallen, full of hunger, war, violence, disease, loneliness, and suffering. We who are privileged, as well as those who live in the poorest, war-torn, and deprived places, came to earth because we had faith that the Savior's Atonement would make our mortal lives worth it. I don't understand why I was born in a time, place, and circumstance of unprecedented opportunity. I only know that the Atonement will somehow remove all such unfairness. In India and Africa the Spirit helped me feel the depth of God's love and find peace, even with the constant presence of poverty, sickness, and suffering. He loves all of his billions and billions of children, most of whom lead difficult and challenging lives, and through the Savior's infinite Atonement, he heals, blesses, and saves us, one by one.

This notion was impressed upon me when one day in Africa we were returning home from a full day of missionary work and were feeling particularly heavy, alone, and tired. As we drove on a backcountry road, we saw a young man wearing a football jersey with "Ostler" (my last name) printed on the back. We stopped and discovered that the jersey was from a football club in Salt Lake City, in an area where my brother lived. A picture and short phone call with my sister-in-law revealed that the jersey used to belong to my nephew, who had donated it several years earlier. Just when we needed it, God reaffirmed that he knew us.

As a part of my growing view of what the Atonement entails, I found meaning in the account of Enoch asking the Lord, "How is that thou canst weep, seeing thou art holy, and from all eternity to all eternity?" The Lord replied, "Behold, these thy brethren; they are the workmanship of mine own hands . . . wherefore should not the heavens weep, seeing these shall suffer?" (Moses 7:31–32, 37). The depth of God's love surprised Enoch—that the Lord would see our suffering and would weep because of it. Fiona and Terryl Givens said of this verse,

> God's pain is as infinite as His love. He weeps because He feels compassion. . . . It is not their wickedness, but their 'misery,' not their disobedience, but their 'suffering,' that elicits the God of Heaven's tears.[3]

(I have always been a bit "weepy" when I think about the challenges of others—I feel encouraged that this is a godly attribute.) Now in my sixties, I better comprehend the reaction of a parent to their child who is suffering. You can't turn away—you can't hide your feelings, and you weep and sometimes sob. If we look, we will see suffering all around us. For some the suffering is physical; for others it is emotional or spiritual. With this understanding, we can reach out and bless those who suffer. Sometimes this ministering is done through our own tears as we become aware of their burdens. At other times it is done through direct service, comforting them in their pain, sadness, and suffering.

God's Expansive Work

Realizing the depth of love God has for all his children, I believe that God works through many, many different means to bless his children. I maintain this belief while simultaneously having faith in the idea that our church is the only church that currently has God's authority and preaches a fullness of the gospel. Latter-day Saints often express this sentiment when they state their belief that the Church is the "only true and living" church. We know, of course, that this doesn't mean we have a monopoly on truth or goodness. I like the words of Samuel B. Hislop, who wrote on the Church's blog,

> Indeed, belonging to the 'only true and living church' does not mean we are the only people doing good or that we're the only group blessed with spiritual insights from God. Our church's interfaith and humanitarian efforts prove we can't do God's work alone—we are, after all, a church of only 15 million in a world of 7 billion.[4]

I have seen God's love work through other people and organizations to teach, lift, comfort, minister, and create faith. My view of God's work is more expansive than I, as a twenty-one-year-old recently returned missionary, could have believed.

In addition to my mission experiences in Africa and India, my career in health care took me around the world. In that job, I worked with people across the globe to strengthen health-care systems, and I saw God's hand working through many of them. One of these was Sangeeta, a doctor from India who had a promising career in the United States but moved back to India to use her skills to train doctors in her home country. I worked with other exceptional people, including Vijay, Susan, Shamsheer, Cheryl, and others, throughout India, China, and the Middle East—people who saw needs and sacrificed wealth and security to make a better life for those around them.

One doesn't have to go to far-flung places to find God working through a variety of people; it happens here at home. Many, many good people sacrifice much to help others. Some feel that their call to serve comes from God, while others are motivated by compassion. I see God's hand in their efforts and am grateful that his work is broader than what can be done by fifteen million Latter-day Saints.

The Book of Mormon speaks of the expansiveness of God's work:

> Know ye not that there are more nations than one? Know ye not that I, the Lord your God, have created all men, and that I remember those who are upon the isles of the sea; and that I rule in the heavens above and in the earth beneath; and I bring forth my word unto the children of men, yea, even upon all the nations of the earth? (2 Ne. 29:7).

I appreciate Philip Barlow's comments on this scripture. He said,

We need not presume our superiority. Rather, we are a people tasked with a commission. We have good news and good ways to share it. This, however, does not preclude the Lord from commissioning others in their own roles. The God of heaven and earth is not so small as any number of clans have presumed. The Church is not the only source of that which is good, true, and beautiful—after which we are invited to seek.[5]

His hand is everywhere.

Stages of Faith Development

These few examples show how my faith has changed throughout my adult life. Our lives are not static. We constantly face new challenges, and it's thus natural and even necessary that our faith changes. The faith of a young child in Primary is different than that of a deacon, whose faith is different than that of a Laurel. Faith development can be a long process, and there are many different paths that process can take in adulthood. One path is not necessarily better than another. As Doctrine and Covenants 46:11 says, "To some is given one, and to some is given another, that all may be profited thereby."

Beginning Stages

There are psychologists who study how religious faith develops. These behaviorists have identified possible stages of faith development. For example, James W. Fowler, a leader in this field, developed a six-stage framework for faith development. As I read Fowler, it became clear that not one stage of faith development is superior to another—stage six is not better than stage three. He uses progressive numbers not to illustrate how faith improves in each stage, but to show the order in which faith tends to change over time.

Here I focus on only the first four of Fowler's stages. Stages one and two occur as we grow up—in our families, Primary, and youth groups. During these stages, we are taught religion by our parents, teachers, and others, and we believe their words.

As we enter stage three, either as youth or young adults, we form our own beliefs; as we say in the Church, we develop our own testimonies. This happens as we grow older and have more experiences in settings such as Church youth groups, seminary, and institute. Eventually we form beliefs that are our own, independent of those of our parents and teachers. Taking ownership of our faith often happens during the teenage years, though sometimes it occurs later, perhaps on a mission. Usually this stage is complete by the time we are young adults. During this period, we develop firm, individual beliefs regarding our religious and spiritual world.[6]

Many Latter-day Saint adults stay in stage three their entire adult lives, having firm confidence in the Church and its leaders. Their faith is meaningful, rich, and vibrant—it defines their lives. For these individuals, their sure faith remains constant, and they can incorporate life experiences and challenges into their existing framework that was formed when they were young.

The Dark Night of the Soul

Mike and Amanda were both in stage three when their beliefs crashed around them. This brought them into Fowler's stage four, which is characterized as a period when people challenge their previous assumptions and assume individual responsibility for their beliefs. For some, this transition results in them completely abandoning their prior beliefs regarding the Church or God, no longer believing in the basic doctrines they were taught when they were young. This transition, according to Fowler, "often brings greater struggles . . . because of its impact upon the more established and elaborated system of relationships and roles that constitute an adult life structure."[7] Thomas Wirthlin McConkie, a developmental researcher, affirms that shifting to stage four "can feel like a full-blown crisis" and "is often harrowing."[8] This stage of faith development is often called the "dark night of the soul," a phrase that comes from the poem of the same title by St. John of the Cross, a sixteenth-century Spanish mystic.[9]

We all have had dark nights. I have had plenty. Joseph Smith cried, "O God, where art thou?" (D&C 121:1). Alma the Younger said, "I fell to the earth; and it was for the space of three days and three nights. . . . I was racked with eternal torment, for my soul was harrowed up to the greatest degree and racked with all my sins" (Alma 36:10, 12). Even Christ himself, in his dark experience on the cross, cried, "My God, my God, why have you forsaken me?" (Matt. 27:46). Though I have not felt these emotions with the same intensity as the prophets or the Savior, I have felt alone at times when trying to magnify my calling, I have felt persecution and the unjustness of others, and I have felt the darkness when I have had to repent.

In a faith crisis, belief breaks, one's shelf of concerns cracks, and one's old faith loses power and meaning. A faith crisis occurs when a person learns or experiences something that significantly challenges their beliefs and they feel they can't trust the spiritual foundation that they had long relied on. This could be a result of encountering new information that conflicts with what they had known, disagreeing with a new teaching or policy, or experiencing personal trauma that causes them to be suspicious of various authorities, settings, or situations. As Thomas McConkie puts it, "A faith crisis points to a kind of falling apart, a disintegration of one's former world that was previously held up by certain beliefs and propositions."[10] In a faith crisis, what a person used to believe and the events they currently experience seem to be at odds with one another, and the person enters a state of intense dissonance and stress. People in faith crises experience emotional turmoil and usually desperately want to find peace. Finding resolution to their questions, however, sometimes results in a loss of faith in some or all of the Church's foundational truth claims. Some don't like the term "faith crisis" because it seems too extreme, but at the same time we shouldn't downplay the deep emotional pain that may come when someone's worldview is overturned, leaving them not knowing what to believe and aware of the deep consequences their crisis may have for their lives, family, and important relationships.

Even people who live Christlike lives can experience a dark night. For years after feeling a direct and personal call to serve the poor, Mother Theresa described in her personal writings the anguish and doubt that she was experiencing. In 1959 she wrote, "In my soul I feel just that terrible pain of loss of God not wanting me—of God not being God—of God not existing." Her "inner turmoil, known by only a handful of her closest colleagues, lasted until her death in 1997."[11] Brigham Young said, "To profess to be a Saint, and not enjoy the spirit of it, tries every fiber of the heart, and is one of the most painful experiences that man can suffer."[12] Like Mother Theresa, Latter-day Saints in stage four live in a night that is dark, lonely, and painful.

Lehi's dream in the Book of Mormon evokes the dark night: "I beheld myself that I was in a dark and dreary waste. And after I had traveled for the space of many hours in darkness, I began to pray unto the Lord that he would have mercy on me, according to the multitude of his tender mercies" (1 Ne. 8:7–8). Lehi passed through the darkness, eventually finding his way out of it. Mother Theresa didn't, though she still held firm to her religious life.

Mike and Amanda had a faith crisis when they encountered aspects of our history that didn't seem to align with what they had been taught most of their lives, and they no longer knew who or what sources to trust.

Their stage-three faith had been built on always trusting and believing the Church and its leaders, but that strategy didn't work anymore for them. Their respective crises impacted Amanda so significantly that she experienced anxiety and depression and had to receive professional help.

For Latter-day Saints in stage four, it can be months or years before they find stable faith footing again, if they ever do. Fowler and other faith development experts agree that those in stage four will never return to stage three—their faith will always be different than before.

Ministering to Those in Crisis

For those who have never had a faith crisis, it can be very difficult to minister to those experiencing a dark night of the soul. Chapters 9 and 10 cover these issues in depth, but first it is helpful to acknowledge the difficulty of empathizing or understanding the darkness, loneliness, anger, and loss others may feel. It may be hard for stage-three eyes to see their stage-four world. Most church meetings and lessons are geared to helping our youth develop their own stage-three faith or to those adults seeking to more confidently live their stage-three faith. These messages don't usually resonate with members in their dark night and may add to their feelings of being alone and misunderstood. For example, we teach that The Church of Jesus Christ of Latter-day Saints is the only true and living church, but we only rarely talk about what this means or how God works through others in accomplishing his work. For those whose questions and struggles have led them to adopt a more expansive view of God's dealings with people, it can seem limiting and narrow when we talk as though we have a monopoly on truth and are the only people God inspires to do good. If we can't help people through their dark night, they may feel they are on their own, lost in the "exceedingly great mist of darkness," and like those in Lehi's dream, they may eventually "wander off" and "lose their way" (1 Ne. 8:23). Indeed, many already have.

We know that some people will leave, but we shouldn't use the imagery of Lehi's dream to give up on trying to address their needs and understand them. I don't think that is the lesson. As God's hands, we are meant to help others find and trust God so that "they [will come] forth and [catch] hold of the end of the rod of iron; and . . . press forward through the mist of darkness, clinging to the rod of iron, even until they . . . come forth and partake of the fruit of the tree" (1 Ne. 8:25). We are meant to help our brothers and sisters through the dark night, but without understanding them, we may inadvertently push them away from the iron rod or make it harder for them to find and hold on to it. Our Heavenly Parents don't want their children alone in the dark night—they want us to be with them, to love them even in the darkness. For a time, we may even need to be the iron rod they cling to. I believe that how we support individuals through their faith crises largely determines their ability to remain engaged as participating, believing (or even doubting) members of the Church.

The darkness and duration of the night will vary depending on the individual. For some, the night is pitch black and lasts for years. But I believe that through our love and understanding, we can bring light to the dark night, making the journey a little easier, and become a bridge that makes passing the night a little shorter. And there are things we can do both as individuals and as a church to help people avoid a crisis of faith in the first place.

Some may be tempted to disagree with what I've said here and view a faith crisis as a simple challenge that can easily be related to. But as I have talked with people who are in a faith crisis or have been through one, I see their challenges as unique. Before I asked questions and truly listened, however, I didn't understand these experiences or feelings and I had little understanding of how to minister to these individuals. In our ministering and efforts to understand those who are struggling with their faith, we should never expect them to return to a stage-three faith—rather, we should walk with them through the dark night, potentially helping them and ourselves develop a new, stronger, and more mature faith, one that reconciles the crisis with its causes.

Still some may disagree with me and feel that I am overdramatizing the pain caused by events that challenge faith, but I feel strongly that those who do not take seriously the charge to mourn with those who mourn, do so at the risk of not understanding and of distancing themselves from the people they love. They are also at risk of not being able to effectively minister. If we don't try to understand, we may increase the burden they carry and the likelihood that they emerge from their dark night with no spiritual belief.

By this point, some readers may wonder what happens to those who enter stage four of faith development. I see two common qualities: First, they prioritize personal responsibility for their own spiritual development over organizational authority. Second, their belief is best described as "nuanced"—their faith is characterized by subtle shades of meaning or expression. I have asked members who continue to believe after a faith crisis about the nature of their faith, and I asked them if the way they now believe has changed. Among the many shared ways their faith has changed, these individuals now:

- Take personal responsibility for their spiritual development, using leaders as valuable reference points along the way.

- Have quiet humility regarding things that once appeared certain.

- Understand historical problems and accept the humanness of leaders.

- Have faith in ambiguity and hold nuanced beliefs.

- Are comfortable with doubt and not knowing everything.

- Have hope in beliefs they once held as absolute truths.

- Find meaning and spirituality in diverse sources, including nature, music, stories, and thinkers outside of the traditional Church canon.

- Identify with spiritual or behavioral thinkers outside of the Latter-day Saint tradition.

- Read scriptures, ignoring historicity, with a focus on personal meaning.

- Value relationships with others regardless of whether they hold the same beliefs.

I know Church members who believe this way without having experienced a dark night, but I know of no members who still believe after a faith crisis who don't exhibit most or all of these characteristics. Their experiences give added meaning to the scripture that says, "For now we see through a glass, darkly," with hope that one day the darkness will give way to light, for "then shall I know even as also I am known" (1 Cor. 13:12).

SECTION 2

TRUST, BELONGING, AND MEANING

For our spirituality and religious affiliation to be strong, they must rest upon a foundation of trust, belonging, and meaning. For faith to run deep, we need to have trust and confidence in what we believe, in the Church where we worship, and in the leaders responsible for teaching and ministering to us. When we participate in church services, we need to feel as though we belong and have the fellowship of other saints. We must share our lives with one another and find ways to support each other as we come unto Christ. We should try to find answers to the most important questions in our lives and find meaning in our worship. Without trust, meaning, or belonging, we may no longer believe as we once did and may seek to find these things in other ways. By understanding how faith is positively and negatively affected, we can find ways to strengthen trust in the Church, help people feel like they belong, and create meaning as we seek for answers to the important questions of life.

CHAPTER 6

Trust

Trust is to a human relationship what faith is to gospel living. It is the beginning place, the foundation upon which more can be built. Where trust is, love can flourish.

—Barbara B. Smith[1]

The primary focus of this chapter is to illustrate how important trust is in the development of our faith and to identify ways that it can be lost. This chapter will also discuss basic principles to help us become trusted ministers to our family members, friends, and ward members who no longer believe.

Losing Trust in Church Leaders

Most of us take for granted the trust we have in the Church and its leaders. Sure, we know that leaders are human and make mistakes and have their own personalities and limitations, but we also know they try their very best to live good lives and to help God's work move forward. Unfortunately, some turn out to be scoundrels who use their positions to harm or take advantage of those they are called to serve, but fortunately such leaders are a rare exception. Over the years I have had a few interactions with general Church leaders, and I have left those meetings universally impressed with their goodness and complete commitment to the gospel of Jesus Christ. I listen to them carefully so that I can learn from them. I trust and have confidence in them. I sustain them.

But many completely lose their trust in the Church and its general and local leaders. In the *Faith Crisis Member Survey*, I asked participants to rate their agreement with three statements:

Rate Each Statement
(*Faith Crisis Member Survey*)

	Strongly Agree	Agree	Disagree	Strongly Disagree
I trust Church leaders.	0%	7%	59%	28%
I am confident in the goodness of general Church leaders.	6%	58%	31%	6%
I am confident in the goodness of local Church leaders.	17%	73%	7%	2%

It almost seems disloyal to report this data, and as I write this I feel sadness that (at least in the group I surveyed) most do not trust Church leaders. Somewhat heartening, however, is that most did seem to believe in the goodness of their leaders, with more trusting in the goodness of their local leaders than in that of the general leadership.

If we were in a conversation with a ward member or friend who said that they did not trust Church leaders or weren't confident in their goodness, what would we say? What would we do? Here are some ways Church members and leaders have responded in the past:

- Expressed concern to the bishop that the person is teaching children in Sunday School or Primary.

- Made sure that their children spent less time at the person's house.

- Warned neighbors that the person was a potential apostate.

- Released the person from his or her calling and took away their temple recommend.

- Testified and expressed heartfelt belief that our leaders are called of God and speak with his authority and on his behalf.

Those who have responded in one of these ways may have had good intentions behind their actions. Perhaps they genuinely wanted to protect their wards and families from what they perceived as a negative influence. These actions, however, usually only further erode individuals' trust, which they were already struggling to maintain, and push them further away.

In the same survey I gauged participants' trust in local Church leaders by asking them to rate their agreement with several statements:

Rate Each Statement
(*Faith Crisis Member Survey*)

	Strongly Agree	Agree	Disagree	Strongly Disagree
My ward leaders know how to effectively minister to individuals in a faith crisis.	0%	4%	41%	55%
I trust my local leaders to guide me through my faith crisis.	0%	1%	37%	62%
My local leaders can help me with the important decisions in my life.	0%	9%	46%	45%
I am comfortable disclosing my current beliefs to my local leaders.	3%	22%	36%	39%
From the outside, I appear as a traditionally believing member of the Church.	24%	54%	18%	3%

Members in a faith crisis do not believe their local leaders will be able to help them and for various reasons choose to keep their doubts and questions hidden. When I asked the *Faith Crisis Member Focus Group* about trust, they taught me that they risk a lot when they talk about their concerns. Here are some of their comments:

> My nickname by which the people in my ward know me now is "the apostate" because I discussed [Gospel Topics Essays] material and discussed non-historicity and allegorical values of scriptures.

> They [Church leaders] are good men for the most part. I do not trust them to understand my angst or have any idea how to deal with it.

> I think Church leaders are generally very good, honest, and sincere. I would also not trust any of them to understand what I am going through because up until I experienced what I have, I would not have known how to respond. My leaders insist that no one will lose their testimony who is reading the scriptures, praying, studying the gospel, going to church—but I do every one of those things, and my testimony of Church truth claims has all but disappeared.

> [I stay silent because of] fear of judgment. I have seen others called out as apostate for having questions, despite being encouraged to have questions from the Church itself.

> I know I would lose the relationships I've developed at church if I were honest, so I pretend.

> Never disclose anything. You will be a pariah. I have learned this the hard way.

One said she worried that her believing husband would be released as a bishop if she disclosed her beliefs. Another feared that her temple recommend would be withdrawn and that she wouldn't be able to witness her daughter's marriage. Another worried that her friendships in her tight-knit Latter-day Saint neighborhood would change. These fears caused them to distrust and be wary of their leaders. Though for the most part these individuals thought their leaders were good people, they did not trust that their leaders would be understanding of their concerns or respond to them in a helpful way.

To illustrate why they feel this way, I want to tell you about Allison, who is in her late thirties and holds a temple recommend. She and her husband are raising two teenage daughters. While she was teaching Church history and the Doctrine and Covenants to teenagers in early-morning seminary, she had questions that led her to studying parts of the Church's early history that challenged her faith. Then, while serving as the Primary president in her ward, she found herself struggling with her belief and wanted help in figuring out how to continue participating in church despite her questions. She felt alone and wanted to discuss her concerns with someone. She didn't feel comfortable going to her bishop, who had earlier dismissed her attempts to introduce the Gospel Topics Essays to ward members and referred to them as "anti-Mormon materials."

She went to the stake president, who strongly encouraged her to talk with her bishop. With some trepidation that doing so would affect her standing in the ward, she and her husband sat down with the bishop. Allison expressed that she "had concerns but was really committed to staying in the Church." She explained that in Young Women, her daughter had discussed how Joseph Smith used a seer stone to help translate the Book of Mormon. Her teacher strongly rebuked her and later told Allison to be more careful in deciding what materials to let her daughter read. The bishop was surprised that Allison had concerns since she appeared to be a completely believing member.

After the meeting, Allison and her husband felt good about both being able to honestly express their concerns and that their bishop had listened to them. However, two or three weeks later, the bishop released both Allison and her husband from their callings without explanation. Allison expressed to her bishop that this was a real setback and that she didn't know how she would participate in church moving forward. Shortly thereafter, a friend of Allison's in the Primary presidency submitted her name to the bishop for approval to call her as a teacher in the Primary. The bishop turned down the sister, telling her that Allison was not worthy.

Allison and her family don't know what to do next. Their oldest daughter is planning on serving a mission, but Allison now feels unwelcome in her ward and has lost trust in her bishop. She and her husband haven't held callings for six months and haven't been invited to participate in any way. They plan to move soon and won't be opening up about their concerns in their next ward.

Having once been called as a bishop, I have great sympathy for other bishops who sacrifice so much of their time and energy to serve those in their ward. Looking back at my own time in the calling, I recognize that I knew very little about the complexities of belief and had a very limited understanding of the challenges of life. I don't know what was in the mind of Allison's bishop, but I can see how a bishop could be fearful, thinking he needed to know all the answers or perhaps that he needed to protect the Church. Bishops and other Church leaders receive very little practical training to help people who have concerns of faith, and often the only strategy they know is to counsel Church members to read the Book of Mormon, pray more, and go to the temple, and in the process believe that they must protect other ward members from what they see as threats to the faith.

It's not difficult to see how Allison's well-intentioned bishop failed her, and unfortunately her experience is not unique. I have, for instance, heard a similar story from a leader's perspective. A Relief Society president in another state told me about two friends who confided in her about their faith crises. Her suggestion to them was to just leave the Church and have their names removed from its records. She then told me it was unclear to her whether she should even assign ministering sisters to them because she felt they likely would not come back. It's probably safe to assume that these two friends no longer trust this leader and likely don't feel welcome to participate.

Building Trust as Church Members

There may not be much we can do to restore an individuals' trust in general or even local leaders, but we can work to become trusted individuals ourselves. Below, I identify several ways we can build trust in our relationships. I believe that these methods are the most important things we can do to build trust as we minister:

- Listen, listen, and listen. Then listen some more—don't rebut, testify, or try to explain away their concerns.

- Ask questions that seek to understand their concerns.

- Don't assume their concerns are a result of sin, laziness, or some other fault—just accept that their concerns are real to them.

- Don't label them with negative terms, such as "doubters," "nonbeliever," and certainly not "apostate."

- Don't tell them how they should feel.

- Keep their concerns in confidence. Don't disclose what they share with you to church leaders or other members without their permission.

- Take steps to address their concerns. For example, if they are concerned about the role of women in the Church, then speak up and work to find appropriate ways for greater involvement and participation by women in your ward and stake.

- Be their voice and advocate on their behalf.

Elder Marlin K. Jensen mentioned many of these elements when he said:

> Often in the church, when someone comes with a bit of a prickly question, he'll be met with a bishop who number one, doesn't know the answer. Number two, he snaps and says, "Get in line and don't question the prophet, and get back and do your home teaching." And that isn't helpful in most cases. So, we need to educate our leaders better, I think, to be sympathetic and empathetic and to draw out of these people where they are coming from and what's brought them to the point they are at. What they have read, what they are thinking, and try to understand them. Sometimes that alone is enough to help someone through a hard time. But beyond that, I think we really need to figure out a way to live a little bit with people who may never get completely settled.[2]

If we can't be trusted to be kind and understanding, members who question will not open up to us. If they feel they cannot confide in us, they will suffer from feeling alone at church. They may work things out on the their own or in a community that will understand them. If they can't trust us, I believe that most will end up leaving completely. One of the central ways through which we can become trusted ministers is by building patience, acknowledging that, as Elder Jensen said, some people "may never get completely settled."

We need to be patient. President Henry B. Eyring said, "Our human tendency is to be impatient with the person who cannot see the truth that is so plain to us. We must be careful that our impatience is not interpreted as condemnation or rejection."[3] We also need to avoid wrongly implying that faithfulness is to unquestioningly follow leaders. From the early days of the restoration, the prophet Joseph taught, "I teach them correct principles, and they govern themselves."[4] We have the responsibility to take the gospel's teachings and apply them to our lives. Terryl and Fiona Givens elaborate on this principle:

> In 1945, a Church magazine urged upon its readers . . . that "When our leaders speak, the thinking has been done." Many are familiar with that expression; fewer are aware that when President George Albert Smith learned of it, he immediately and indignantly repudiated the statement. "Even to imply that members of the Church are not to do their own thinking," he wrote, "is grossly to misrepresent the true ideals of the Church." Regrettably, this myth persists in the minds of many Latter-day Saints, even as leaders disavow infallibility and urge upon members personal responsibility.[5]

When a leader implies or explicitly stresses following without thinking, they will lose the trust of those who understand the principle of self-governance and any who have doubts or questions.

James is a bishop who understands faith crises and has been able to help people retain faith while they have been in their dark nights. I asked him how he helped, and he said,

> The first thing I did was to bring a bookshelf into my office and display some of my books, especially biographies of prophets and other classical books. I wanted to send the message that I was a well-read bishop and that studying the gospel and reading Church books was my passion. I wanted the members to know that I knew my stuff so that when I would counsel them, they knew I knew what I was talking about. This I believe made a huge difference among those intellectual members who were having a faith crisis. They knew they could trust me.

A member in this bishop's ward wrote me and explained: "My dear Bishop had conversations with me often. He gave me blessings so many times, visited me countless times and listened to my pain." Because of the trust that this member had in James, he can fully participate, not with the stage-three belief he once had, but with belief nonetheless, and a recognition of the Church's goodness.

Building Trust on an Organizational Level

In both the *Local Leader Survey* and the *Faith Crisis Member Survey*, I asked participants about the training provided to local leaders about faith crises. I asked them to rank their agreement to three statements:

Rate Each Statement

	Local Leaders Survey		Faith Crisis Members Survey	
	Strongly Agree	Agree	Strongly Agree	Agree
The Church as a whole provides adequate information for leaders to help people who are in a faith crisis.	10%	43%	0%	1%
Our stake and ward provides training to leaders about faith crises.	2%	13%	0%	1%
My ward leaders know how to effectively minister to individuals in a faith crisis.	1%	25%	0%	1%

Even with their confidence in general Church leadership, local leaders recognize that they are on their own in understanding how to respond to today's challenges of faith. And clearly Church members with questions lack confidence that their leaders can help them. Our leaders need more materials, with explanations on how to use them, to help meet these challenges.

That being said, I think we can use our councils to find effective ways, a topic which I cover in depth in Chapter 10. Even if we aren't a member of a stake or ward council, we can counsel with others in our family, Relief Society, elders quorum, or even with those to whom we minister. We can discuss how to build trust and minister to those who have questions and to find effective responses. All we have to do is take the time to put it on the agenda, to invite people who have concerns to educate us, and to be humble in responding to what they say. Although it requires real effort to really learn and understand, if we continue with our lack of understanding, our efforts to help will seem hollow and uninformed, reinforcing the belief that we can't be trusted.

If a leader chooses to ignore or dismiss other points of view, they will lose the trust of those they are called to serve. Leaders carry tremendous power—power to permit temple attendance, to label someone as worthy, and to accept and call members to lead or teach. When they are not cautious about that power, they can inadvertently harm, offend, and lose the trust of others. Looking back on my days as a bishop and stake president, I can see things I learned over time that created more trust in leaders and the Church in general. Here are a few:

- Praying to know which Church members understand modern challenges of faith and could be called to serve in leadership.

- Proactively asking millennials, particularly those concerned with LGBTQ and women's issues, to be involved in leadership, teaching, council meetings, sacrament meetings, and other teaching settings.

- Using councils to identify key faith issues that may need attention and inviting those with unique perspectives to provide input and advice.

- Using a teacher council meeting to address methods of teaching that create trust, belonging, and meaning for class participants.

This is just a small sampling of what can be done with the tools we have in our wards. A comprehensive discussion is found in Chapter 10.

One member in the *Faith Crisis Member Focus Group* shared an experience of having a bishop who encouraged her to be involved, even with her faltering faith:

> I trust my bishop. I know he has experienced a faith crisis and is still in. He chooses to see the goodness of the people he serves, despite historical issues

or current policies. He wants to bring diversity of thought and inclusion of all people to the ward. He asks the questions: How can I make people's lives better? How can I lift others? He took a risk by asking me to serve as the Relief Society president even though he knows my doubts and my intense struggles. He is truly a good man. I believe it is rare to find a bishop like this, and I'm very fortunate. Without him, I'd be one step closer to sending my resignation in.

The ability to help those in our wards and stakes is not limited to bishops and other priesthood leaders. Whether we are in a leadership position or not, it's clear that there are things all of us can do to adapt the above list to our own circumstances in our families and in any calling in which we serve. I know several people who do not have formal leadership callings but who are sought out as persons who can be trusted because they understand the issues that challenge faith and can empathize, accept, love, and comfort those who are struggling.

Tailoring Trust to the Individual

For each person, trust is created differently. I am an older white man who has been a local Church leader and is generally not intimidated by people with formal authority. I retired early with a good income. I have never been sexually assaulted or harassed and never needed treatment for mental health. In short, I am privileged. I am in the minority. It's easy for me to open up and trust my leaders, but for others it's not. The way we build trust with women, minorities, sexual assault survivors, those who suffer with mental illnesses, the poor, and the physically sick may be different based on their circumstances. Each situation is different, and each person is unique. I hope that as you have read this chapter, you understand how important trust is and how it can be easily lost, particularly regarding issues of faith.

In Chapter 5, we discussed how leaders can make mistakes, usually with the best of intentions. With this awareness, I now take a greater responsibility for my own decisions. I listen to my leaders and know they have sought God's inspiration as they give me their best advice. But I take responsibility for deciding how, or if, that advice applies to my life. General leaders don't know me or my situation, but they have been set apart and have spiritual gifts that can help me come unto Christ. I recognize that maintaining trust is a two-pronged effort. If we as Church members set our leaders on a pedestal and believe they are always right, we may lose trust when we see them make mistakes. And if leaders aren't humble about their limitations, they may lose our trust.

In addition to the thoughts expressed in this chapter, section 3 outlines specific ways we can become trusted, but the endeavor always starts with the same basic steps: coming to understand people through studying and listening, being respectful, keeping confidences, and withholding judgment.

CHAPTER 7

Belonging

It is always surprising if you keep your mind open and your heart open. You find out lots of wonderful things about people that you might not have ever expected. But when you've experienced, when you've seen, when you've opened your heart to other people you see that we all belong.
—Jean B. Bingham[1]

Through song, we teach our Primary-aged children about the importance of belonging. The message of the song is simple, connecting us to the Church, to our Heavenly Parents, and to our Savior Jesus Christ:

> I belong to The Church of Jesus Christ
> of Latter-day Saints.
> I know who I am.
> I know God's Plan.
> I'll follow him in faith.
> I believe in the Savior, Jesus Christ.
> I'll honor his name.
> I'll do what is right;
> I'll follow his light.
> His truth I will proclaim.[2]

This song is one of the first songs taught to children in Primary. From the beginning, belonging to the Church is a crucial part of our Latter-day Saint identity.

Understanding Belonging

But what is belonging? Brené Brown, a popular researcher on the topic, explains belonging by contrasting it with the related but lesser concept of "fitting in." "Belonging is being accepted for you," she writes. On the other hand, "fitting in is being accepted for being like everyone else. If I have to be like you, I fit in."[3] In my family, I don't have to hide my beliefs and behaviors out of fear of being rejected. I don't "fit in" with my family—I belong. I can be goofy and tell dad jokes, I can be emotional and shed tears or express anger, and I don't have to hide that I secretly read the daily avalanche forecast for the Utah mountains because I love the power of nature and grew up powder skiing. Most importantly, I can be honest about my faith, hopes, and doubts. I can be authentic with my family, even in my weaknesses.

But once I venture out the door of my house, I become more guarded. I put up a shell and protect those parts of myself that I am concerned might not be accepted. I don't show my vulnerability, my weaknesses, or my limitations. Even at church, I am careful to show my best self. I dress and act the part people expect of me, even in those moments when I don't feel it. Even with the confidence that I have in our Heavenly Parents' plan, I find myself guarded when it comes to those areas where I have hope instead of belief. I feel vulnerable and am cautious of looking different. This isn't feeling that I truly belong.

We all want to belong. We all want to feel loved and wanted, even with our weakness and limitations. My spirituality is my foundation, and therefore it is essential that I feel that I belong in the Heavenly Family and in the Savior's church and in my own ward. I believe the same is true for others.

Belonging at Church

In the *Faith Crisis Member Survey*, I asked members if they felt they belonged:

Rate Each Statement
(*Faith Crisis Member Survey*)

	Strongly Agree	Agree	Disagree	Strongly Disagree
I feel like I belong in my ward.	2%	32%	50%	17%
I feel like I belong in the Church.	1%	19%	55%	25%
I can be authentic with my ward about the major issues in my life.	1%	8%	42%	50%
My ward accepts me as I am.	2%	44%	44%	10%
My personal differences divide me from others at Church.	30%	58%	12%	0%
I want to belong to the Church community if I can be who I am.	38%	51%	8%	1%

I have spent a lot of time thinking about the data in this table. It seems clear that these Church members do not feel like they belong in their wards, nor in the Church at large. But they want to. Here are some of the comments given in the survey that explain why some Church members with unorthodox views feel they don't belong:

When I've been more open, I've been shut down. For example, in a Sunday Relief Society meeting, when the lesson was about basic gospel doctrines, I asked to add polygamy to the list on the chalkboard. The Relief Society president said, "Let's keep things happy!" I also got that look from a couple of sisters of why do I want to cause problems? If I express my honest feelings, I feel more and more like an "other" and a service project. People are overly friendly, but it comes from "now we have to fellowship her back into the fold" kind of love.

I disagree with some Church beliefs and policies. I feel if I speak up, I would be attacked and disregarded.

Leaders [see] questions as unacceptable criticism.

[There is an] unspoken rule that you must agree (or at least not verbalize disagreement) with the narrative in the room.

There is no space for different interpretations of the theology; there is no space for real Church history; there is no space for my questions; there is no space for an empowered knowledgeable woman's voice; a man will just override her thoughts. Being open in the Latter-day Saint faith doesn't make me feel closer to God; it makes me feel separated.

People would be scared of me [if I expressed my real opinions].

[I don't want] to upset others who are still believing. [I don't want] to turn over any apple carts, so to say.

These members clearly feel that that they neither fit in nor belong and that their differences are not welcome. Indeed, any differences we have—not just those related to faith—can potentially lead to feelings of not belonging. I suspect that it's not just their differences of faith that trigger these feelings but that a large percent of believers also feel this way. There are many things, including incomes, marital status, sexual identity, political views, ways we interpret gospel teachings, and lifestyle choices, that divide us and cause us to feel that we don't belong.

At church, just like other places, there can be a pressure to assimilate and be like those around us. Some of this pressure is cultural—we all have grown up with an idea of what the ideal Latter-day Saint looks and acts like. In an interview with Terry Givens, Elder Marlin K. Jensen said,

I don't think we do well by those that don't fit our norms. The young man who doesn't serve a mission or who comes home early; the person struggling with same-gender attraction; the divorced woman—those who are different. I think if you meet the norm, if you're striving for the ideal, and you're coming close to it, I think Mormonism is a glorious place to be. If you're not—if you're in some in-between state where you don't quite fit—I don't think we've learned yet quite how to bring that person in.[4]

Doubting once strongly held beliefs is another way people may not seem to fit the ideal. Responding to the sense of isolation that some feel for not believing the same as those around them, Givens in another interview discusses how we need to make our community more welcoming to those who lack strong belief: "We need to decriminalize doubt. . . . Even for those of us who are certain of the underlying foundational tenants of our faith . . . [i]t is incumbent upon us to shape the culture that characterizes [the restored gospel of Jesus Christ]."[5]

We as members define the culture within our wards (as well as our families), and based on the data above, it seems we have a culture that does not extend belonging to these members. Church classes aren't meant to be graduate courses in history, science, sociology, or psychology, and church shouldn't be a place of controversy where every point mentioned is debated. But people come to church to find peace, meaning, and hope, and I am hopeful that we as members can find ways to welcome those who struggle with belief but still come to find those things.

Belonging at Home

It's not just at church where members without full belief feel that they don't belong. They often feel this way in their homes and families, where they most ought to feel like they belong. We are a family-oriented religion. Family is a core part of our doctrine, and for many of us it is the basis of our culture and everything about our lives. Families can differ in many ways, but home is the place where we expect and hope for love, acceptance, and peace. We believe families can be eternal, and our personal hope is that our family—whatever shape it takes—will be with us forever.

We as Latter-day Saints take pride in our families and what they represent. When a family member stops believing, it threatens our goals, hopes, and even our identity. Proverbs 22:6 says, "Train up a child in the way he should go; and when he is old he will not depart from it." I don't interpret this verse the same way I used to. To me, this scripture is not a promise that a child won't stop believing if raised in the gospel, but rather it is motivation for parents to live our lives according to Christ's precepts with confidence that the Atonement will provide healing and salvation to all who ultimately come unto him. This scripture shouldn't cause us to second-guess our parenting but should give us motivation to be more

Christlike in all our family relationships, especially with family members who no longer believe.

I, myself, have family members who have lost their testimonies of the doctrines of the Church. For me, there are empty chairs in the temple. My wife and I don't fully understand how the Atonement applies to our "empty chairs," but we have confidence in the potential that comes from the infinite love of our Heavenly Parents. Although our lives are subject to eternal laws like agency, my wife and I believe that through the Atonement our family will be whole. We have said to ourselves and to our family members, "No matter, no matter, no matter, no matter, no matter what . . . we will love you." My wife and I have made mistakes, and there are words and actions that I wish I could take back. However, showing these family members our complete love has not been difficult, and we haven't felt tested in our willingness to fully accept and embrace them— even without the belief they once had, even when they make what we consider to be bad decisions, and even when they do things we wouldn't. I hope and pray they feel like they belong in our family.

Our home has no empty chairs at the dinner table. No matter.

I don't have all the answers and don't pretend to be the gold standard of family relationships. I'm just like many of you, trying my best to figure it out as I go. It's not always rosy for believing family members, even when they try their best to be loving and accepting. But I have learned that some who no longer believe also feel intense pain in their homes; they can experience family rejection at a time when they need support the most.

I interviewed Roger, who is twenty-nine and experienced a faith crisis about three years ago. He is a returned missionary and was married in the temple. His faith crisis was sudden, and he found himself not believing in a matter of days. In just two and a half weeks, he and his wife separated, and he became estranged from his parents. His parents rejected him. His mother, father, and wife never wanted to understand what led to his no longer believing—he was left alone in trying to understand his own faith.

Because of these family challenges and his faith crisis, he became depressed and attempted suicide. His parents said that he could no longer live with them. His mother sends him regular text messages letting him know that he is worthless and that the troubles in his life are due to him rejecting his faith. He is divorcing and sees his children only periodically, and he has reason to think it's because he no longer believes in the Church. He doesn't put all the blame for the situation on his family, and he recognizes that he has made mistakes. Regardless, he is now estranged from his family and knows his relationships with them will likely never be based on love.

I include this story to illustrate how a faith crisis can impact a whole family. Roger's relationships with his ex-wife, children, and parents will never be the same. Each person involved has their own story—I am sure they all feel deep pain because Roger no longer believes.

Creating Places of Belonging

When we face a challenge like Roger's family's, our best course is to find a private place to process our grief and do everything we can to find ways to show love. Tom Christofferson, brother of Elder D. Todd Christofferson, wrote about the acceptance he received from his family when he came out as gay over thirty-five years ago. He quotes his mother recalling the decision they knew they had to make:

> I thought we really had it all figured out, that we were the perfect Mormon family. But then life happens, and I realized that there is no perfect Mormon family. The only thing we can really be perfect at is loving each other.[6]

As the Christoffersons were planning a family reunion, they learned that Tom wanted to bring his boyfriend. As they counseled as a family, his mother addressed his siblings, some with young children, and told them: "The most important lesson your children will learn from how our family treats their Uncle Tom is that nothing they can ever do will take them outside the circle of our family's love."[7] At about the same time, his brother Wade shared a similar sentiment: "We don't understand or know how all of this will play out in eternity, so we are going to make sure we enjoy every single moment with Tom in this life."[8] I admire this family for expressing true Christlike love and not letting their uncertainty get in the way of their relationship with their son and brother.

Building a bridge of love leads to belonging. Have confidence that our Heavenly Parents love your nonbelieving family member completely and have the hope that comes from the Atonement. In his October 2013 General Conference address, President M. Russell Ballard spoke on our duty to embrace those who struggle with belief and make sure they know they belong:

> My heartfelt plea is that we will encourage, accept, understand, and love those who are struggling with their faith. We must never neglect any of our brothers and sisters. We are all at different places on the path, and we need to minister to one another accordingly. Just as we should open our arms in

a spirit of welcoming new converts, so too should we embrace and support those who have questions and are faltering in their faith.[9]

A month earlier, when speaking to Latter-day Saints in Southern Utah, President Ballard shared similar sentiments, saying,

> We have heard stories where someone asking honest questions about our history, doctrine, or practice were treated as though they were faithless. This is not the Lord's way. . . . We need to do better in responding to honest questions. Although we may not be able to answer every question about the cosmos or about our history, practices, or doctrine, we can provide many answers to those who are sincere.[10]

I've wondered why we are so quick to put down divergent views. It might be rooted in our persecuted past, in the exclusive view we hold of the restoration of the gospel, in our view of the eternal battle between good and evil, or perhaps in fear that others' doubts will somehow harm our family or our own belief. Whatever the reason, judgment and criticism too often seem to permeate our culture, causing people to feel as if they cannot belong.

If fear is at the root of our tendency to be unwelcoming or wary of people who don't believe like we do, then we have some work to do. Fear will never lead to a sense of belonging. The Zen priest Joan Halifax said,

> All too often our so-called strength comes from fear, not love; instead of having a strong back, many of us have a defended front shielding a weak spine. In other words, we walk around brittle and defensive, trying to conceal our lack of confidence. If we strengthen our backs, metaphorically speaking, and develop a spine that's flexible but sturdy, then we can risk having a front that's soft and open. I believe it comes about when we can be truly transparent, seeing the world clearly, and letting the world see into us.[11]

To truly be welcoming and help others know that they belong, we must be willing to be vulnerable ourselves—just as they are when they choose to remain despite their uncertainties that set them apart.

I have confidence in the gospel plan and believe that when we truly understand the depth of our Heavenly Parents' love, we will be overwhelmed by it. My love for my children is deep, but it is still a far cry from the love of God. According to Elder Orson F. Whitney, "Our Heavenly Father is far more merciful, infinitely more charitable than even the best of his servants, and the everlasting gospel is mightier in power to save than our narrow finite minds can comprehend."[12] I am not fearful of the truth or the plan. I have confidence in the love that brought about the Creation and is at the core of the Atonement. Because of that confidence and security, I also feel confident that we can find more ways to help people authentically belong.

In addition to combatting our own fears and developing confidence in the love of our Heavenly Parents, we can create places of belonging by making concerted efforts to be open with others and their experiences. Sister Jean B. Bingham, general Relief Society president, has also spoken on the importance of being open to others. She said:

> Until you have seen people who are different from you in lots of different ways, I think it is easy to get focused on a very narrow segment and feel like that is the only way to be. . . . One of the best ways to form a good relationship is to not come in with assumptions or preconceived notions, keeping an open mind, an open heart. Sometimes we tend to pigeon-hole people, or we assume that they are a certain way because of a certain situation in their life or their family. It is always surprising if you keep your mind open and your heart open. You find out lots of wonderful things about people that you might not have ever expected. But when you've experienced, when you've seen, when you've opened your heart to other people, you see that we all belong.[13]

All Church members ought to feel that they belong. Whether they are gay, straight, Republican, Democrat, childless, single, divorced, educated, black, Native American, poor, young, or old—or whether they have doubts—we want all to sing with authentic feeling "I belong to The Church of Jesus Christ of Latter-day Saints." If we accept the responsibility of making our homes and church meetings more welcoming and loving places, withholding judgment as much as we can, then we will have taken a major step forward in building a bridge that those in a faith crisis will want to cross.

CHAPTER 8

Meaning

[Religion] can go into a world in which there is a great deal of pain and
suffering and loss and bring meaning and purpose and peace.
—Rabbi David Wolpe[1]

Meaning That the Gospel Provides

An essential element of being human is finding meaning and direction in our lives. We long to know who we are, where we come from, and what our purpose is. I think deep down all of us want to find meaning and purpose. I found this poem that expresses the longing I imagine most of us share:

> To learn while still a child
> What this life is meant to be.
> To know it goes beyond myself,
> It's so much more than me.
>
> To overcome the tragedies,
> To survive the hardest times.
> To face those moments filled with pain,
> And still manage to be kind.
>
> To fight for those who can't themselves,
> To always share my light.
> With those who wander in the dark,
> To love with all my might.
>
> To live a life that matters,
> To be someone of great worth.
> To love and be loved in return
> And make my mark on Earth. [2]

The restored gospel of Jesus Christ teaches rich, eternal truths that can help us find meaning, peace, and direction in our lives. As individuals and scholars who explore these doctrines, Fiona and Terryl Givens are powerful voices in helping Latter-day Saints who question find meaning and belief. I've heard them teach about the uniqueness and power of the doctrines restored through Joseph Smith and others. In their writings, the Givenses provide helpful insights that build upon what is discussed in our basic church classes, and they have helped me appreciate the true revolutionary message of the gospel.

In their book *The God Who Weeps*, the Givenses outline five unique doctrines of the gospel:

1. God is a personal entity, having a heart that beats in sympathy with human hearts, feeling our joy and sorrowing over our pain.

2. We lived as spirit beings in the presence of God before we were born into this mortal life.

3. Mortality is an ascent, not a fall, and we carry infinite potential into a world of sin and sorrow.

4. God has the desire and power to unite and elevate the entire human family in a kingdom of heaven and, except for the most stubbornly unwilling, that will be our destiny.

5. Heaven will consist of those relationships that matter most to us now.[3]

In Primary, we start teaching these unique and amazing doctrines in a simple Primary song:

> I am a child of [Heavenly Parents]
> And [they] have sent me here,
> [Have] given me an earthly home
> With parents kind and dear.
> Lead me, guide me, walk beside me,
> Help me find the way,
> Teach me all that I must do
> To live with [them] someday.[4]

I know of no other religion that teaches all these truths—that defines the essence of meaning, direction, and purpose in these ways. We teach that we are divine, that salvation is open to all (regardless of when and where we live), that we can have eternal relationships after this life, and that our potential is to become like our Heavenly Parents. This expansive view of humankind gives me hope that despite my weaknesses, I am of worth to my Heavenly Parents.

The way each of us finds meaning in our lives is unique. Our background, culture, education, and life experience all define what is meaningful and important to us. I have lived alongside the poor in rural India, the hyper-rich in London, the destitute in Sierra Leone and India, and now the upper middle-class in my neighborhood in Virginia. I have seen how the meaning we look for may have differences, but it is universally sought.

But regardless of the kinds of problems we face, we all have at least one thing in common. In every place I've been to, almost everyone I have met wants to find meaning in their lives.

Jana Riess's research sheds light on how Latter-day Saints of different generations may find meaning in different ways. She asked Latter-day Saints living in the United States to identify the top issues facing America today. She stratified the answers based on generation. For boomers and the silent generation, the top issue was "moral or religious decline," selected by 41 percent of respondents. But for millennials, it was only the third most-important issue, with only 27 percent selecting that option. The top issue for millennials was "poverty/hunger/homelessness," selected by 30 percent of respondents, while this was the sixth most-important issue for boomers and the silent generation, with 21 percent selecting that option. "Changing views on the traditional family" was tenth for millennials but fifth for boomers and the silent generation.[5] This demonstrates that the young look for meaning in different ways than those who are older; overall young people think more about issues like racism, sexism, environmental concerns, poverty, sexual harassment, and gun violence than older generations. These differences in viewpoints between the younger and older generations may be a result of differences in both life experience and stage of life. Social scientists are unclear whether millennials will adopt older generations' values as they age, but just as the Great Depression, World War II, and the Cold War permanently shaped the boomers and silent generation, millennials will always carry the impact of the war on terrorism, unprecedented political divisiveness, and the Great Recession.

Women and men generally see the world differently and often find meaning in different ways. Yet despite all these differences the restored gospel universally provides meaningful answers to our most basic questions of identity and purpose and offers a deeper understanding of what is of most value in this life.

Losing Meaning at Church

Fortunately, the doctrines that the Givenses outline and others that are commonly taught in church can provide meaning to almost everyone. That meaning, however, is not felt by everyone who attends church. In the *Faith Crisis Member Survey*, I asked participants about the meaning they found at church:

Rate Each Statement
(*Faith Crisis Member Survey*)

	Strongly Agree	Agree	Disagree	Strongly Disagree
Prior to my faith crisis, Church doctrines were spiritually meaningful to me.	51%	39%	8%	1%
I feel like Church doctrines are spiritually meaningful to me.	2%	44%	44%	10%
The Church addresses the spiritual issues that are most important to me.	1%	19%	55%	25%

Almost all these members found meaning in the Church's doctrines prior to their faith crisis. For some, that meaning has faded; for others, it has been lost. But most concerning is that these members do not feel that their spiritual concerns are being addressed within the Church.

We have all been to meetings where the speakers were ill-prepared and gave boring talks, and we have probably all sat through simple and repetitive lessons read straight from the manual. While there are multiple strategies to find meaning and value in these situations, those who responded to my survey are pointing to something different. For these members, they long for meaning and direction but struggle to find it at church.

What is at the root of people's longing for meaning? What are they looking for? What isn't there?

Many members who find themselves no longer believing or who are unsure what to believe are looking for ways to move forward in the Church and in developing their faith. They are deciding what they believe or are trying to find peace amidst the newfound uncertainty about their beliefs. For some, their past world is shattered, and they are alone trying to find their way. Can they still believe in God? Can they trust Church leaders? Do they belong in our community? How will they raise their children? What does it mean for their temple marriages? Will their family and friends reject them? The questions are individual and endless, and they are at the heart of one of my favorite Latter-day Saint hymns:

> Where can I turn for peace?
> Where is my solace
> When other sources cease to make me whole?
> When with a wounded heart, anger, or malice,
> I draw myself apart,
> Searching my soul?

Where, when my aching grows,
Where, when I languish,
Where, in my need to know, where can I run?
Where is the quiet hand to calm my anguish?[6]

Finding Meaning at Church

While there may be several reasons why some of our brothers and
sisters stop finding meaning in the Church, we need to be willing to look
in the mirror to see if part of the problem lies with us. In 1955, Rabbi
Abraham Heschel discussed what he saw as one of the reasons for the
decline of religion in the twentieth century. He said,

> It is customary to blame secular science and anti-religious philosophy for
> the eclipse of religion in modern society. It would be more honest to blame
> religion for its own defeats. Religion declined not because it was refuted,
> but because it became irrelevant, dull, oppressive, insipid. When faith is
> completely replaced by creed, worship by discipline, love by habit; when
> the crisis of today is ignored because of the splendor of the past; when faith
> becomes an heirloom rather than a living fountain; when religion speaks
> only in the name of authority rather than with the voice of compassion—its
> message becomes meaningless.[7]

Our institutional worship is effective when it is interesting and com-
pelling because it speaks to the issues that we face. I believe the living
foundation that Heschel refers to is the message that helps us endure our
challenges and provides answers to the problems we see in our lives and
the lives of those around us. Finding meaning is more than developing
a belief in a God and a Savior; meaning exists when we can find reason
and purpose in the challenges we see in society. But we all see the world
differently, and the issues that matter to one may not matter to the other.
Some issues are well-addressed by the Church; others are rarely discussed.

For example, we regularly discuss the importance of having a strong
family in society, but we rarely discuss how to eliminate racial discrimination. We are quick to talk about the need to take care of the poor through
fast offerings and humanitarian aid, but we rarely talk about the wors-
ening wealth and structural inequalities that exist in society. We rightly
try to keep politics out of our meetings, but for many, social justice and
equality are essential principles of the gospel of Jesus Christ. Still others face heavy burdens of more temporal issues, including mental illness,
loneliness, poverty, sexual identity, racism, divorce, and suicide. We rarely
discuss these, but almost every one of us has experienced these problems

personally or in our families. We want to know how the gospel helps us with those challenges and how it provides answers and teaches us how to minister to others.

Perhaps we need to broaden the topics that we cover at church and to be more honest about the challenges of the human experience. I asked the *Faith Crisis Member Focus Group* how we should create more meaning at church. The question quickly sparked a discussion about how to be more effective at expressing love, compassion, and vulnerability. The group provided several examples of instances where they found meaning at church because of the honesty of certain members:

> A well-kept, seemingly has-it-all-together man got up during a lesson on addiction recovery and held up his one-year sobriety chip and offered his witness of how the gospel had helped him through rough times and how he knew he could not do it alone and needed help and support.

> During a heated debate on whether we should give money to panhandlers, a woman in her sixties or so who everyone knows and loves shared her heartfelt story about once being homeless and on drugs and how she felt guilty about taking money and using it for alcohol but it got her through one more day and she eventually found hope through the charity of others and the gospel to change her life.

> An elders quorum president started one lesson with a heavy sigh and an honest "this week was hard for me."

After we talked about the need for authenticity and belonging and discussed how those attributes provide meaning and connection, we discussed the need to focus more on Christ. The fellowship most of us want at church is understanding how our real lives, challenges, and joys connect us together through the teachings of Christ. One participant sad:

> I've been through entire meetings where the only mention of the Savior was the "in Jesus name, Amen" at the end of prayers. We have way too much "follow the prophet," "pay your tithing," "go to the temple," and a host of other peripheral distractions, and not anywhere close to enough talk about Jesus Christ, Savior and Redeemer, and the core values he taught. He's an afterthought in this church, no matter how much we want to crow about our name!

This comment sometimes hits close to the mark. I too have sat through a number of sacrament and other church meetings in which there hasn't been any mention of Christ, his life, or what it means to be Christlike. In those meetings, an investigator from another Christian church would leave without any evidence that Christ is at the center of our faith. When our discussions connect Christ's teachings to our real, everyday lives, we find meaning.

Meaning doesn't come from just one thing—it comes from the gospel in its entirety. We should talk about tithing and following the prophet, but we should also talk about issues of fairness and equality. We should talk about keeping the law of chastity, but we should also talk about sexual harassment and the sexism that remains in society and even in the Church. We should talk about reading the scriptures and praying daily, but we should also talk about how to cope with mental illness and how to support each other through personal tragedy, including divorce, addiction, or suicide. For some, because of their circumstances, meaning may feel further away. We need to find ways, for example, for LGBTQ members, single members, and those of different cultures to know how they can feel meaning in their lives.

Returning to the hymn "Where Can I Turn for Peace?" the remaining lines poignantly identify where this meaning and relevance can be found:

> Who, who can understand?
> He, only One.
>
> He answers privately, Reaches my reaching
> In my Gethsemane, Savior and Friend.
> Gentle the peace he finds for my beseeching,
> Constant he is and kind,
> Love without end.

SECTION 3

MINISTERING

This last section asks us to examine ourselves. It would be easy to put the book down now and think that with our new insights, we know how to make a difference in how we approach those who no longer believe or have faith. But these next chapters help us go a step further. They hold a mirror up to ourselves so we can examine, in specific terms, what we can do better or differently to make a lasting, helpful impact in our ministering to those we care about.

CHAPTER 9

Key Principles of Ministering

Often, what is needed most is for us to be prayerful and to listen without giving advice or platitudes. People who are suffering don't need our explanations for their condition. Our well-meaning attempts to put the situation in perspective (our perspective) can unintentionally come across as demeaning or insensitive.

—Ann E. Tanner[1]

"Ministering" is a holy term that describes how we watch and care for each other and how we show the love of our Heavenly Parents. The Church defines it as "learning of and attending to others' needs. It is doing the Lord's work. When we minister, we are representing Jesus Christ and acting as His agents to watch over, lift, and strengthen those around us."[2] Jesus Christ is the example. "Jesus wept" when he ministered to Mary (John 11:35). Though he knew he would resurrect Lazarus, he chose to stop and, without giving a sermon, take the time to cry with her as she mourned the loss of her brother. On the cross, while undertaking the infinite Atonement, he looked beyond his own unimaginable suffering and saw the needs of his anguished mother and assigned the apostle John to care for her by simply saying, "Behold thy mother" (John 19:27). He saw the infinite worth of the woman taken in adultery when he said, "Neither do I condemn thee" (John 8:11). As recorded in the Book of Mormon, he showed universal compassion when "he did heal them everyone as they were brought forth unto him" (3 Ne. 17:9). In his ministry, Jesus mourned and forgave, protected and healed—he showed love and compassion. Coming unto Christ means seeking to minister as he does.

People experiencing a faith crisis often feel loneliness and isolation. For many of these individuals, their entire lives have been built upon a belief in the Church, and when that foundation becomes wobbly or disappears completely, all their church-based personal relationships are at risk. The resulting loneliness they feel makes connection even more important. According to Brené Brown,

> We believe that the most terrifying and destructive feeling that a person can experience is psychological isolation. This is not the same as being alone. It is a feeling that one is locked out of the possibility of human connection and of being powerless to change the situation. In the extreme, psychological isolation

can lead to a sense of hopelessness and desperation. People will do almost any-thing to escape this combination of condemned isolation and powerlessness.[3]

Ministering means being the human connection that people in this isola-tion need.

Modern scripture teaches us that the power to minister does not come from being a parent or from having a calling or assignment. Nor does it come through priesthood office or authority. As Doctrine and Covenants 121 teaches us, "No power or influence can or ought to be maintained by virtue of the priesthood." Power in ministering comes "only by persuasion, by long-suffering, by gentleness and meekness, and by love unfeigned; By kindness, and pure knowledge, which shall greatly enlarge the soul without hypocrisy, and without guile" (vv. 41–42). Ministering is loving people and developing authentic relationships. And it doesn't require a perfect knowledge of the gospel or of others' lives. Eric D. Huntsman in a devotional at Brigham Young University explained this well when he said,

> As aspiring Christians but still imperfect Saints, we may not always un-derstand the struggles of others or know how to help. But we can always love them, creating safe spaces where others—and often we ourselves—can struggle with the hard sayings in life.[4]

Either we can help build trust and belonging for people or we can push them away. The way we treat others determines the level of their trust in our relationship with them and our professed belief in Christ. If they trust us, they are more likely to be who they really are—to be authentic—with us and to feel a sense of belonging. As we better understand why people leave the Church and the intense emotions they feel during the process—including feelings of anger, fear, and loss—we don't have to agree with their decision to distance themselves from the Church, but we can feel and express empathy for them and their changed belief. To them, the is-sues that concern them are real, and their feelings are deep.

Although we should always hope that everyone will find the meaning, belief, and connection we have in the restored gospel of Jesus Christ, if our ministering is based only on that hope, our efforts will likely be shallow and ineffective. We should instead set our expectations on building deeper and more loving, complete, and accepting relationships. When our min-istering is based on compassion and acceptance, people are more likely to trust us and to open up about issues that are important to us both. In this chapter I focus on three essential principles of ministering that will help create trust and connection: listening, avoiding alienating behaviors, and creating loving relationships.

Listening

If we want the kind of relationship that Huntsman described in his devotional, we must strive to understand others. This starts with listening. As James the brother of Jesus taught, "Let every man be swift to hear, slow to speak, slow to wrath" (James 1:19). Following this pattern, listening builds trust and helps others feel confident in our sincere interest and comfortable in sharing their important and vulnerable parts. We need to let others tell us about their struggles, concerns, and beliefs. When we feel the time is right, we can ask questions such as:

- Do you mind telling me about what led you to step away from the Church?
- How has your belief changed over the last year?
- Why have you stopped attending church?
- Tell me about what you believe.

Shortly after his resurrection, Jesus exemplified these types of open-ended questions as he ministered to two disciples who seemed to be having their own struggle of faith with the news of Jesus's death. On the road to Emmaus, he asked the unknowing disciples, "What manner of communications are these that ye have one to another, as ye walk, and are sad?" (Luke 24:17). He then let his disciples talk, and he listened. We can follow the Savior's example and do the same, even if what others say may be hard for us to hear. We don't want to hear negative things about beliefs or doctrines we hold dear, and we may see things completely differently from the person we are talking to, but we shouldn't let negative or uncomfortable feelings keep us from seeking to understand.[5]

One remarkable example of ministering through listening comes from Fred Rogers—better known as Mr. Rogers—whom multiple generations of children watched and learned from in the second half of the twentieth century. Rogers carefully designed his show to communicate to children at their pace and in a way that created a calm and safe space, even as he covered complex issues, including death, divorce, race, and war. To understand these issues from a child's perspective, he spent time on and off the show listening to children. A journalist visited him in 1995 to understand the success of his program. The interview became personal, and Rogers opened up about the grief he was experiencing after losing one of his best friends. After talking, Rogers said to the journalist, "You're ministering to me, Tim. By listening you minister to me." The journalist later wrote,

"Fred wanted to know the truth of your life, the nature of your insides, and had room enough in his own spirit to embrace without judgment whatever that truth might be."[6] In other words, Rogers wanted to truly understand people. Watching Mr. Rogers with my grandkids and learning more about him, I see the amazing way he connected with others and showed love—and at the heart of that connection and love was listening.

The power of listening and understanding that Rogers exemplified was studied by Ralph G. Nichols, who started his career as a high school speech teacher and debate coach. As he worked with student debaters, Nichols found that they improved their persuasive ability when their listening skills improved. Based on this observation, he completed a PhD with a dissertation on listening behavior. Listening became his life-long academic pursuit, and he became known as the "father of listening." His work led him to create the International Listening Association, and he published one of the first scholarly books on the importance of listening, *Are You Listening?*[7] Through his research Nichols learned that many lack the skill to effectively listen, and he identified ways to teach others to learn better and develop better relationships. Speaking of the importance of listening, he said, "The most basic of all human needs is to understand and be understood. The best way to understand people is to listen to them."[8]

When we truly listen, we gain not just an intellectual understanding of someone else's thoughts but also a deep, emotional connection to the other person. At the end of almost all my interviews with those who have had a faith crisis, I have been thanked for listening and letting them tell their stories. Their gratitude surprised me. These experiences reminded of the popular quote: "Listening is an attitude of the heart, a genuine desire to be with another which both attracts and heals."[9] Most of the people I interviewed will likely never meet me in person, but for them there was something important, helpful, and healing about being heard.

The integral connection between listening and healing was explained by Thích Nhất Hạnh, a Vietnamese Buddhist monk:

> Deep listening is the kind of listening that can help relieve the suffering of another person. You can call it compassionate listening. You listen with only one purpose: to help him or her to empty his heart. Even if he says things that are full of wrong perceptions, full of bitterness, you are still capable of continuing to listen with compassion. Because you know that listening like that, you give that person a chance to suffer less. If you want to help him to correct his perception, you wait for another time. For now, you don't interrupt. You don't argue. If you do, he loses his chance. You just listen

with compassion and help him to suffer less. One hour like that can bring transformation and healing.[10]

In my interviews with mostly distant strangers, I found Nhất Hạnh's observations to be true. After being given a safe environment to share their authentic thoughts and after being truly heard, these individuals, to whom I was a virtual stranger, felt better. They received a measure of compassion and healing. Imagine the healing we could provide to the people we know and love if we were to really listen to them.

Janet Dunn experienced this kind of healing. She was serving in a Christian ministry when she suffered severe emotional fatigue that forced her to return home. "I knew I needed help," she said.

> Scared, yet desperate for answers, I made my way to the office of a Christian counselor. At first, my answers to his questions were guarded. But as I noticed his compassion and understanding, I began to feel safe. Soon words were pouring out of me as he sat listening intently. Like broad strokes of a paintbrush, my words were recreating whole scenes—memories of past incidents, areas of confusion. His perceptive questions helped me describe my feelings, many of them deeply buried. Talking with someone who cared gave me a chance to hear my own thoughts, and it was the beginning of my cure.[11]

Janet began a life-long pursuit of learning how to listen. Looking back on her experience, she says, "I learned that listening affirms people. Indeed, it is one of the highest forms of affirmation. When we listen, we invite another person to exist." Listening and allowing people to talk helps them clarify their thoughts and find ways to sort through the challenges they face with someone who supports them.

Psychologists, marriage counselors, and life coaches spend much of their careers helping other people learn to listen and communicate effectively. Here are some tips I have gleaned from some of these experts as I have studied how to be an effective listener:

- Be ready to listen: find the right space, time, etc. Put away the phone and turn off the music.

- Show care through body language and tone of voice and by smiling and making eye contact.

- Throughout the conversation, give brief verbal responses, such as "Okay" or "I see," to show you are listening.

- Avoid giving advice.

- Instead of asking "yes" or "no" questions, pose open-ended questions and statements, such as "Tell me more," "How did you feel?" and "What was it like to experience that?"

- Allow for silence. If needed, say, "Give me a minute please. I want to think about how to respond."

- Do not switch the conversation back to you—be present for them.

In interviewing and talking with people who no longer believe, I found some common themes. At the beginning of a discussion, those I have spoken to almost always have initial reservations about sharing their experiences and feelings. They often spend some time gauging my purpose and sincerity. For example, I met with a man in our stake who had stopped attending church meetings about twenty years ago. He agreed to meet with me and tell me why he stopped going. We knew each other a little, but we didn't have deep rapport. As the conversation continued, I sensed reservations in his willingness to be open. I asked him whether he had a concern that my real reason for talking with him was to get him to return. He smiled and said that he had thought that. I reassured him that I just wanted to understand why he no longer attended. Reassured, he gradually became more willing to share with me some significant and personal experiences and feelings. I was surprised at his degree of openness since we barely knew each other.

This experience has happened time and again. In my conversations with individuals who struggle with the Church, they have been open and honest, but they make it clear that they are not always so forthcoming. I asked them why they haven't talked with others about their faith or feelings. Their concerns are wide-ranging, though there are some commonalities. Everyone seemed to be concerned about confidentiality. Their stories and their feelings are theirs alone, and they have the right to control who gets to hear them. They are also afraid of being misunderstood, judged, or labeled. These issues of faith and belief are intense and important for them, and they worry that others will minimize their concerns. By opening up, they risk a lot, including their social and family relationships. We saw this with Amanda in Chapter 5, whose relationship with her mother has never been the same since her faith change, and Allison and her husband in Chapter 6, who were released from callings after Allison confided with her bishop about their struggling testimony. Some have slowly lost close friendships after being open and honest about their faith challenges. Even without the fear of repercussions, others may also be hesitant to express their thoughts and feelings out of a worry that the other would rather argue with than listen to them or because they want to protect the listener from information that might unsettle them.

These individuals probably have many more concerns than those listed here. If we want others to speak to us openly and honestly, we must do our part to relieve their concerns and fears. We can do that by being completely sincere and caring when talking to people about their thoughts on belief and the Church. Here are some statements that have the power to reassure people and allay their concerns:

- No matter what you say, I will love and respect you.

- I understand you have different beliefs, and it won't change our friendship.

- I will do my best to understand your perspective and your feelings.

- I promise to keep this conversation confidential.

- I will just listen. I won't preach, give advice, or tell you that you are wrong.

- Tell me why you are concerned about telling me about your beliefs.

- Even if you hold different beliefs than I do, I know you are a good person.

- I love you.

Each situation will be different, but these statements are examples of how to frame our conversations in ways that will be affirming and build trust in our relationships, and they should remind us that the purpose of listening is to build understanding. As we listen and build authentic relationships, more of us will feel like we belong. However, for those who have a strong belief in the Church and its teachings, listening to those who have lost that belief can sometimes be challenging. Some may have concerns that are uncomfortable to think or speak about, and we may be unsure of how to handle them. If we don't want to talk about a particular issue because we think it could shake our own faith, we can try to focus the conversation on the other person's feelings and not the details of their concern. If the conversation goes into too much detail on a controversial issue, we can acknowledge that they seem to be well-studied, and though they may know more about that topic than we do, we understand the gist and want to focus the discussion on how to strengthen our relationship with them and better understand how to support them in their beliefs.

It's also helpful to keep in mind that although a person's concerns may be triggered by a few controversial issues, at the core of all of these concerns are usually a loss of trust, belonging, and meaning—which we can at least partly address with expressions of love and empathy.

Because of the intensity of their feelings, some may become angry as they open up and talk about their experiences. In most cases, validating and accepting the importance of their concerns will help them set aside their anger. At other times, they may just need to vent. For many going through a faith crisis, their anger may be sharply directed at the Church or our deeply held beliefs, making it difficult to be an effective listener. In these situations it is important to not take the anger personally, and it may be appropriate to tell them that we care about the Church and our faith and to ask them to try and respect our beliefs while we strive to understand theirs.

As we seek to build or maintain a trusting relationship that creates a sense of belonging, our friend or family member may test us to see if we are willing to let them be authentic. I have found that some may test the waters, disclosing information slowly to see how we react. They may want to see if we will cut off discussion when a controversial issue comes up, or they may become angry to see if we turn away. Their caution or anger may be a way to see if talking to us will risk their friendship, status, calling, or our respect. To assuage their fears, we need to affirm our constant love and acceptance of them at each step and test.

The more we listen, the more we will understand and empathize. We will build trust and increase their confidence in our relationship with them, removing the isolation that so often comes to those who no longer believe. And as we listen, we often must leave our comfort zone to show compassion, love, and understanding.

Listening means that we see people as they are. We recognize and respect their right and position to hold opinions and beliefs that are different than ours. In *The Anatomy of Peace: Resolving the Heart of Conflict,* the authors show how conflict can originate when we view and treat others as objects that we can control or manipulate, that are irrelevant or mere obstacles, or that have value insofar as they can be vehicles for our own objectives. On the other hand, when we treat others as persons with genuine and important hopes, needs, cares, and fears, their hopes, needs, cares, and fears become more relatable and important to us. It's easy to slip into viewing another as an object. When paying a cashier at a store or calling a customer service representative on the phone, it's easy to see the persons assisting us as mere objects or tools to get us the items and services we want. When a mistake happens or when things take longer than we wish, we too often become angry or frustrated and begin to see these persons as obstacles in our way or wasters of our precious time instead of persons with families, needs, feelings, and imperfections.

In our relationships with people who believe differently, we too may lose sight of the person and think of them as a disruptive problem, a threat to the hopes we have for our family, or an embarrassment to our image of a perfect family. We may see them as an assignment to somehow get them to believe differently. Some church leaders may view a person as a thirty-minute appointment keeping them from other things they want to do. When we view people in this way, we are thinking of them as objects. *The Anatomy of Peace* describes the damage that treating people as objects can cause: "Seeing an equal person as an inferior object is an act of violence. It hurts as much as a punch to the face. In fact, in many ways it hurts more. Bruises heal more quickly than emotional scars do."[12] Someone we perceive as a disruption or problem is a person with divine worth with agency to choose who merits acceptance and acknowledgment that their circumstances are real and important. Listening shows our respect for the other person.

Avoiding Alienating Behaviors

As we minister through listening, there are behaviors that we can adopt that are helpful and others that are potentially hurtful. Some things we do make listening ineffective; some behaviors may even damage our relationship with others. I remember hearing the story of six-year-old Sally, who asked her father where she came from. Her father gave an extended explanation of the birds and the bees, after which Sally, perplexed, said, "Tommy comes from Pittsburg. Where do I come from?" This benign story of not understanding a question before answering is contrasted by the hurtful experience Allison had with her bishop, who I assume tried to listen but didn't fully invest himself in trying to understand. As a result, Allison and her husband felt alienated from their ward and the Church.

Formulating a Response Instead of Listening

Stephen R. Covey observed, "Most people do not listen with the intent to understand; they listen with the intent to reply."[13] If this is a habit most of us have, we must break it in order to show love and develop understanding and empathy. When hearing someone talk about their faith struggles, our intention may be to change the person or how they view the Church. We must, however, set aside those intentions if we want to truly listen. This is hard in any setting, but when it comes to religious topics we hold dear, listening to understand and not persuade can be even harder. We may distract ourselves from listening by silently praying for just the right thing to say. Such prayers reflect our faith but may pull us away from listening intently with the goal of feeling empathy, showing love, and developing understanding. At other times, instead of listening, we may spend the time the other person is talking looking for openings to testify of truths we believe. In other cases, when we hear how someone feels about controversial issues, we may be hurt, uncomfortable, or fearful and draw away. But listening means to be completely present, not spending our focus on our own feelings or formulating a response to the other person's statements. As we read in Proverbs, "He that answereth a matter before he heareth it, it is folly and shame unto him" (18:13).

Preaching and Giving Unwanted Advice

Our tendency in conversations to focus on formulating a response instead of listening is often connected to a desire to give others counsel that we believe will help them. Our purpose in listening, however, should be to understand others, not to convince them to change. Speaking of those who are experiencing challenges to their faith, Latter-day Saint author Adam Miller writes,

> To help them, I don't need to show up at their door to tell them what ought to keep them up at night. I need, instead, to listen. I need to let them tell me what keeps them from sleeping. I need to let them tell me what worries and frightens them. And in response, even if I don't share that worry, I need to be ready and willing to mourn with them as they mourn.[14]

If we are speaking to persuade or are focusing too much on our own point of view, then we are not truly listening—or ministering.

In a recent BYU devotional, President M. Russell Ballard similarly cautioned against the tendency we have to speak rather than listen to those going through a faith crisis. In answer to the question, "If I have family or friends who are less active, how far do I go in my attempts to bring them back?" he said,

> My answer is please do not preach to them! Your family members or friends already know the Church's teachings. They don't need another lecture! What

they need—what we all need—is love and understanding, not judging. Share your positive experiences of living the gospel. The most powerful thing you can do is share your spiritual experiences with family and friends. Also, be genuinely interested in their lives, their successes, and their challenges. Always be warm, gentle, loving, and kind.[15]

A crucial part of listening and forming connections with others is, as President Ballard emphasizes, caring in others' lives, not instructing or judging.

The scriptures often mention the importance of calling people to repentance. Reading or speaking about the early chapters of 1 Nephi often evokes the image of the prophet Lehi standing in front of a group of angry people and telling everyone how wicked they are. Perhaps there is a time and place for this kind of rebuke, but it is not when we are trying to build an understanding relationship with a family member or friend. The most effective way to cry repentance is to try to minister and build relationships as Christ would and to be examples of love and acceptance.

Reflecting on my experiences in leadership callings, I see many times when I didn't listen as I should have. I thought my calling was to counsel, teach, correct, and testify, and while those roles are important, I now realize I should have been a better listener. I remember praying to know what to say or which scripture to quote to help, but now I see I should have been praying to feel what the other person was feeling and to better understand how to more fully love and comfort them. I'm sure there are people who left a discussion with me who didn't feel heard and didn't think I really wanted to understand. I certainly didn't help them rebuild their trust in the Church. I am sure that some lost confidence that local leaders could help them, and I am sure that some lost faith because I choose to give them advice instead of listening to their concerns.

For Church leaders, parents, or other figures with power or formal or informal authority (including those who are older and, in some cases, those who feel they have authority by virtue of being male), listening can be harder. With all the right motivations and intentions, some of these individuals may feel they have a role or experiences that give them insight into others' lives, the right to critically evaluate what they hear, or the responsibility to give advice. They may think they have heard it all and stop listening. Or perhaps they feel they can use their experience, age, gender, or role to push the other person to believe differently. In either case, trust is lost, and the relationship isn't strengthened and may even be weakened. People who have authority, whether real or perceived, may need to be especially careful and self-aware to become accepting and understanding listeners.

Social scientists have repeatedly shown that giving advice isn't a helpful way of building a relationship.[16] When we need a good listener, most of us are looking for empathy, understanding, and connection, not counsel. I remember coming home from work one night, and my wife needed a listening ear. Her day was difficult and full of challenges. As she relayed to me the problems of the day, I started problem solving. Kindly, she stopped me and said, "I just need you to listen." She just wanted me to be there with her. Parker Palmer, a Quaker elder and educator, eloquently summarizes this point: "The human soul doesn't want to be advised or fixed or saved. It simply wants to be witnessed—to be seen, heard and companioned exactly as it is."[17]

Turning the Conversation to Ourselves

Sometimes in our desire to develop rapport with another person, we turn the conversation to ourselves in a misguided attempt to show empathy. Here is one story to illustrate:

> A good friend of mine lost her dad some years back. I found her sitting alone on a bench outside our workplace, not moving, just staring at the horizon. She was absolutely distraught, and I didn't know what to say to her. It's so easy to say the wrong thing to someone who is grieving and vulnerable. So, I started talking about how I grew up without a father. I told her that my dad had drowned in a submarine when I was only 9 months old and I'd always mourned his loss, even though I'd never known him. I just wanted her to realize that she wasn't alone, that I'd been through something similar and could understand how she felt.
>
> But after I related this story, my friend looked at me and snapped, "Okay, Celeste, you win. You never had a dad, and I at least got to spend 30 years with mine. You had it worse. I guess I shouldn't be so upset that my dad just died."
>
> I was stunned and mortified. My immediate reaction was to plead my case. "No, no, no," I said, "that's not what I'm saying at all. I just meant that I know how you feel." And she answered, "No, Celeste, you don't. You have no idea how I feel."
>
> She walked away, and I stood there helplessly, watching her go and feeling like a jerk. I had totally failed my friend. I had wanted to comfort her, and instead, I'd made her feel worse. At that point, I still felt she misunderstood me. I thought she was in a fragile state and had lashed out at me unfairly when I was only trying to help.
>
> But the truth is, she didn't misunderstand me at all. She understood what was happening perhaps better than I did. When she began to share her raw

emotions, I felt uncomfortable. I didn't know what to say, so I defaulted to a subject with which I was comfortable: myself.

I may have been trying to empathize, at least on a conscious level, but what I really did was draw focus away from her anguish and turn the attention to me. She wanted to talk to me about her father, to tell me about the kind of man he was, so I could fully appreciate the magnitude of her loss. Instead, I asked her to stop for a moment and listen to my story about my dad's tragic death.[18]

My daughter recently had a similar experience at church. She serves with others in her ward's nursery, and one of the other workers told her his wife was in the hospital because of a postpartum infection. With concern for his wife and managing four kids and a newborn at home, he expressed that he was overwhelmed. Shortly thereafter, my daughter watched as another man came into the nursery. He told the husband that he was his new ministering brother and asked what he could do for him. The husband said, "I have had a hard weekend." The ministering brother responded with, "Me too. It has been crazy." The conversation ended there. Ministering means we are present—listening, validating, and focusing on the other person. When we do otherwise, we become the fool described in Proverbs: "A fool hath no delight in understanding, but that his heart may discover itself" (18:2).

Labeling

Understanding that words matter, the Savior said, "Whosoever shall say, Thou fool, shall be in danger of hell fire" (Matt. 5:22). Clearly, the Savior was not in favor of placing labels on people, but following his example can be difficult at times since our minds are wired to categorize the people and things they see. To help us make sense of the world, our brains categorize and separate, for example, what we like to eat from what we don't, things that are flat from those that are round, and the color green from the color red. These labels are helpful, allowing us to store and retrieve information and to take what we know about one thing and apply it to something else with the same label.

This helpful function of our brain, however, can also be harmful, since it is often easy for us to minimize the importance of people and their ideas by applying simple labels to them, placing them into tidy boxes. Sometimes we use labels to help explain away a person, idea, or experience we haven't taken the time to understand; we turn people into simple caricatures who are exclusively defined by a simple word or phrase. But people are far too complex to label with a single term, and we will never know enough about them to accurately judge their behaviors and actions.

I've heard labels applied to those who no longer believe in the Church, and these labels are almost always harmful, dehumanizing, and inaccurate. One member of the *Faith Crisis Member Focus Group* express it thus: "Labels are the trump card that forbids honest inquiry, prevents discussion with loved ones, and endorses the judgmental labeling." Here are some examples of such labels:

- *Apostate.* This label is synonymous with traitor, defector, deserter, and turncoat. It rarely describes the kind of person who simply loses faith, and it is hurtful to those to whom it is applied. Using this term will never draw someone back to participation or involvement or build trust or belonging.

- *Anti-Mormon.* This term was first used to describe the mobs trying to drive the Saints out of Missouri and is commonly used today to describe persons perceived to be attacking the faith. However, it is too often applied to label those whose faith is simply different than that of active members of the Church. Some people may be ardent in expressing their concerns about faith, but I think their sometimes harsh tone is usually a result of not feeling heard. The overuse of this label is obvious when it is unfortunately not uncommon to hear Latter-day Saints even mistakenly call Church-produced material (such as the Gospel Topics Essays) "anti-Mormon" when it presents information that differs from their own understandings.

- *Feminist.* This term isn't as clear cut. For many, this term equates to providing respect and opportunity to women that so often has been culturally denied. For others, it symbolizes an agenda of women ordination, toppling male leadership, or even of man hating. When it is used as a label it is almost always used with a negative stereotype. I have heard it applied to people, usually women, who see that women can and should be more equally engaged in the Church and its leadership or to mothers who don't have a traditional stay-at-home life. Because of the term's negative connotation that some give it, this label shuts down conversation and discussion and minimizes those who it is applied to. One comment from someone who participated in the *Faith Crisis Member Survey* said, "It's incredibly challenging to be a single adult member of the Church. The difference between how I'm perceived in the world, as a powerful woman who runs an organization, and how I imagine people perceive me at church can be jarring." If we label her a *feminist* as a way to not hear her concern, we will fail to understand how she feels.

Other painful labels identified by the *Faith Crisis Focus Group* include "too educated," "fence-sitter," "deceived," "unfaithful," "faithless," "confused," "weak," "cafeteria Mormon," "doubter," "antagonist," "in left field," "infection," "lazy," "intellectual," "fallen," "fallen elect," "nonbeliever," "lukewarm," "goat," "agitator," "heretic," "black sheep," "on the road to apostasy," and "gone to the dark side." In my experience, I have found that it is not just the labels that hurt; they are often said with a tone intended to minimize, exclude, or shut down a person. Labeling someone sends a message to them and to others to behave and believe in a certain way, or else they too will be labeled, categorized, and judged.

Not all labeling is perhaps done maliciously. We label and categorize in part to help us make sense of something that is new. Put a new vegetable on a kid's plate and they will react without tasting it the same way they have reacted to other vegetables in the past. In a similar way, we might use labels to help us make sense of someone who no longer believes because the situation may be new to us. Because we don't understand it, we label it to help us understand. We label something in order to make it fit into our current worldview, since that is easier than questioning our own perspective. It takes a real mental shift to remain open-minded and to not accept our minds' tendency to label.

Judging

As is the case with labeling, we are naturally inclined to make judgments, often without full understanding. Speaking at BYU's Women's Conference, Sandra Rogers, then dean of the College of Nursing at BYU, talked about how judgement can get in the way helping others. She said,

> Humility and charity help us serve without making unrighteous judgments. We do not need to know how or why the person we are serving got into that situation in the first place. We may trust that "what God hath cleansed, that call thou not common" (Acts 10:15). The great form of charity may be to withhold judgment.[19]

She then relays the story of Lisa Flindt, a graduating senior from BYU who wrote about overcoming judgment:

> Taking care of AIDS patients has made me take a hard look at my values. Though I have always felt the individual to be of infinite worth to our Father

in Heaven, I have never before associated with people who were experiencing trials so different from mine and who needed Heavenly Father's infinite love so much. I learned the deeper meaning of charity when I cared for a wheelchair-bound HIV patient. He had lesions on his hands and buttocks, was pale as a ghost with a splotchy red rash consuming his body, and wore dark sunglasses which made him seem even ghastlier. His partner sat at his bedside. Initially, looking at the men made me feel physically ill. I wanted to hold my breath, toss the patient his gown, and spend as little time in the room as possible. However, one day his mother entered the room. When she went to him, kissed him on the forehead, and whispered, "Sweetheart, I will never leave you," the words *charity never faileth* came to mind and my soul melted.[20]

Lisa's soul melted when she saw the love of this patient's mother. When we are judgmental of people's conditions, choices, or beliefs, our perceptions become distorted and we lose the ability to be sympathetic. Judgmental comments often apply a general moral or personal conclusion and are typically based on a person's limited experience. At the surface, faith may seem simple, but faith is shaped by one's culture, personality, life experiences, and individual spirit. Although our natural tendency is to make sense of others' beliefs in terms of our own beliefs, without spending the time to listen and really understand, it's virtually impossible to evaluate what someone really believes or how they came to those beliefs. Just as Lisa's soul melted when she saw the love of her patient's mother, the love of our Heavenly Parents for all their children should help us overcome our tendency to immediately judge others and help us develop understanding and trust.

The following judgments are commonly applied to those whose faith in the Church has changed. By critically examining them, we can stop perceiving people in simple and often lazy ways and open ourselves to building strong relationships based on respect and understanding.

- *Choosing offense.* In October 2006, Elder David A. Bednar counseled Church members to choose not to be offended. This is wise counsel because we are capable of recognizing our feelings, choosing how to respond, and deciding to forgive and set aside wrongs that may have happened to us. But even though Bednar's words are good counsel, when we are listening and building a relationship of trust with others, we shouldn't tell them what to think or feel. By telling people that they are choosing to be offended, we minimize how they feel and often inflict more hurt. We should let God be the judge and understand that our role is just to minister.

- *A hidden sin.* In our attempt to understand someone's changed faith, we may believe there is a secret or hidden sin that explains why the person lost the Spirit. In almost all of my interviews and in the *Faith Crisis Member Focus* Group, these types of sins never came up. But almost universally, these individuals felt that others judged their faith crisis to be the result of sin, laziness, or lack of personal spiritual behaviors such as scripture reading, prayer, or temple attendance. We can't judge the reasons why someone no longer believes. Instead, we should accept the reality of their belief and feelings and be loving and Christlike.

- *Tares to separate ourselves from.* This comes from the parable found in Matthew 13:24–30 about the separation of the wicked and righteous in the last days and is often applied to people who no longer believe traditional Church teachings. When we examine the parable, the tares are traitors planted to choke the wheat. When we label someone as a tare, we judge that their behaviors and beliefs are evil, trying to destroy our belief and that will one day be removed and burned. Do we really believe that? Do we believe these people are expendable? That they are weeds? That the Church will be better off without them?[21] We certainly don't believe that God has given up on them, but calling them tares implies that perhaps we have.

These kinds of judgments are surface-level ways to explain a person's loss of belief, and they frequently involve other hurtful behaviors, including ignoring, excluding, and gossiping. The antidote to judging is finding ways to understand others and build authentic relationships.

Manipulating

The 1944 film *Gaslight* is about a husband whose wife suspects him of criminal activities. In an attempt to convince her that her suspicions are irrational, he systematically begins messing with her mind with the hope of causing her to believe that she has lost a grip of reality and cannot trust herself. He takes a brooch from her and says she must have lost it. He hides a painting and says she took it. Soon the woman begins to doubt her reality, perceptions, and sanity. The term "gaslighting" comes from the 1938 play of the same name and refers to a form of manipulation wherein someone tries to make another doubt and question their memories or perceptions. Gaslighting can include direct manipulation as well as denials and misdirection to try and convince someone to change their beliefs. The term also refers to attempts to make someone's behaviors or experiences seem wrong or defective because of mental issues or other limitations.

Generally, few of us intentionally manipulate or gaslight others; however, we sometimes still do so unintentionally through our communications. For example, I know a sister who expressed concern upon learning for the first time that Joseph Smith used a seer stone in a hat while translating much of the Book of Mormon. Another sister dismissed her concern, pointing out that this fact had appeared in Church publications for years. By responding this way, the second sister is gaslighting the first by implicitly dismissing her concern as dishonest, irrational, imaginary, or stupid. We may inadvertently manipulate others in similar ways when we say things like "Everyone knows that" or "I can't believe you think that" or "What a crazy idea" or "We never believed that." When we truly and respectfully listen, however, we avoid dismissing others' concerns or trying to change their minds, and we never manipulate, either purposefully or accidentally. We should focus our attention on letting them know we love them and care about them and on being interested in what they believe and feel. The restored gospel provides sacred insight into agency and a person's right to choose their own beliefs; we should never try and manipulate someone to believe a certain way.

Knowing When to Stop

Our desire and efforts to understand our friends and family members shouldn't become an irritant in our relationship with them. We should look for clues that will let us know whether additional listening and discussing is helpful. In some cases, ministering may be simply accepting the other person and letting them guide the relationship, at least when it comes to aspects of their belief. They may just need to know we are there for them and love them. They may not want to open up or feel that a fundamental disagreement could get in the way of their overall relationship with us. We shouldn't push them to talk about things they don't want to talk about. If you can't tell from their body language or other hints that they want to talk about their beliefs or experiences, just ask them. You can say, "I am always here to listen if you want to talk about what you believe and why." Then, if they don't want to talk, we can respect their choice and strive to be there for them in other ways. Whether we are a local Church leader, family member or a friend, we should always let them decide how much they want to disclose about themselves and how much they want to be understood.

Creating a Loving Relationship

Listening and accepting the person for who they are is the first step in building loving, ministering-based relationships. Another important step in ministering to others and building relationships is feeling deeply the love that our Heavenly Parents have for each of their children. Elder Dale G. Renlund expressed this truth beautifully:

> I now realize that in the Church, to effectively serve others we must see them through a parent's eyes, through Heavenly Father's eyes. Only then can we begin to comprehend the true worth of a soul. Only then can we sense the love that Heavenly Father has for all of His children. Only then can we sense the Savior's caring concern for them. . . . This expanded perspective will open our hearts to the disappointments, fears, and heartaches of others.[22]

While visualizing this divine love, our relationship with others takes on a new dimension. We see the hope that our Heavenly Parents have for them, expressed in a patient eternal plan and an infinite Atonement.

Beyond listening, there are other actions we can take to recognize and feel the love of our Heavenly Parents for those whose beliefs are different than ours. These actions include expressing empathy, building positivity, and validating; by practicing and implementing these behaviors we can strengthen our relationships and build a bridge of understanding.

Expressing Empathy

So where do we start in helping our friends and family? According to Elder Jeffrey R. Holland, the answer is empathy. "Sounds pretty inadequate," said Holland, "but it is a place to start. We may not be able to alter the journey, but we can make sure no one walks it alone. Surely this is what it means to bear one another's burdens."[23] We must show others love and compassion and let them know our relationship with them is stronger than their changed belief.

Empathy is at the core of ministering. It's at the core of successful relationships, whether in a marriage, at work, or with friends and family. The author Roman Krznaric describes empathy as

> the ability to step into the shoes of another person, aiming to understand their feelings and perspectives, and to use that understanding to guide our actions. This is what distinguishes empathy from kindness or pity, emotions and actions that may be well intended but are often more about the self than the other person. As George Bernard Shaw pointed out, "Do not do unto

others as you would have them do unto you—they might have different tastes." Empathy is about discovering those tastes.[24]

Ministering may start with listening, but to be truly effective it must move further and include support, comfort, mourning, and love—in short, empathy. This is at the core of the Savior's teachings, explicated in the commandment to "love thy neighbor as thyself" (Matt. 19:19). In that short commandment, we are instructed to love others with the same level of understanding as we do ourselves. We are not simply to love and serve another; we are to understand with our hearts who they are and what their fears and concerns are, just as we understand ourselves and our own thoughts. As Jesus wept with Mary and Martha (John 11:32-35), declared the woman with an issue of blood healed (Luke 8:43-48), and physically touched unclean lepers (Matt 8:1-3), he exemplified empathy by understanding what each individual needed most and offering it to them.

Just as Jesus expressed empathy in each situation, we must also attune ourselves to the different needs of others. While empathy starts with listening and withholding judgment, it goes deeper to understanding the feelings behind the person's words. Brené Brown writes,

> Empathy is a strange and powerful thing. There is no script. There is no right way or wrong way to do it. It's simply listening, holding space, withholding judgment, emotionally connecting, and communicating that incredibly healing message of "You're not alone."[25]

Empathy means we can feel what is in the other person's heart. We know—not just in our brains, but in our hearts—their challenges, pains, sorrows, and joys. Though there may not be one best way to show empathy for another person, we can work on developing certain traits that will help. Roman Krznaric, for example, explains that great empaths have curiosity about other people; they want to know how others tick, and they use their curiosity to put themselves in others' shoes. Empaths also examine their prejudices and try to find common ground. They find ways to build connection, which often leads others to open up about their own challenges and vulnerabilities. It takes effort, but empathy is a skill we can develop.

Part of showing empathy is letting others be in pain if that's what they are feeling. We show more support if we acknowledge that their pain exists and join them in their pain than if we were to try to cheer them up. We must acknowledge things are as bad as they think they are. It's rarely possible to talk someone out of their pain. If we try, they will usually stop telling you about their pain, though they will still feel it. To hear, "Yes, this hurts," without someone trying to talk them out of their feelings—that is what helps. Acknowledgement makes things better, even when they can't be made right.

Building Positivity

All successful relationships are based on a foundation of positivity. This principle is illustrated in research done by John Gottman and Robert Levenson, who studied what makes marriages successful. They observed couples addressing contentious problems and systematically evaluated positive and negative communications. They were able to predict with 90 percent accuracy which couples would stay together and which would divorce. The researchers concluded that

> the difference between happy and unhappy couples is the balance between positive and negative interactions during conflict. There is a very specific ratio that makes love last. The magic ratio is 5 to 1. This means for every negative interaction during conflict, a stable and happy marriage has five (or more) positive interactions.[26]

Though this conclusion is specific to marriages, we can apply the findings to strengthen all of our relationships.

Highlighting the importance of positive interactions during disagreement, Gottman and Levenson's research indicates that we don't have to avoid difficult issues with others in order to have a positive relationship.[27] Even in moments of conflict or disagreement, we can find ways to be positive. We can build positivity, for example, through laughter, gestures, giving a hug, holding a hand, or putting an arm around the other person. We can use affirming words like "I understand," "I can see how you feel that way," and "I'm so sorry." These all help create a positive relationship. After revealing that positivity during conflict is one of the best predictors of successful long-term relationships,[28] Gottman and Levenson go on to outline five strategies that can help increase our positive interactions with others and avoid behaviors that are negative:

- Avoid the escalating negativity, including criticism, defensiveness, contempt, and stonewalling.
- Don't become irritable.
- Don't become emotionally disengaged.
- See things optimistically instead of negatively.
- If you feel fearful or want to flee, take a short break or find a way to relax; we don't process information well with high emotions.[29]

The strategy seems pretty simple—we need to make the foundation of our relationships positive and make sure negative interactions don't define how we relate to one another. Of course, there are all sorts of barriers to having the 5-to-1 magic ratio, including those discussed previously such as judging, labeling, giving unwanted advice, not being present, and manipulation. Other common barriers to building strong relationships lie in our differing perceptions, which can be shaped by our gender, life experiences, cultural background, or age. When a discussion includes the topic of faith, other barriers may arise such as fear for the welfare or salvation of the other person. On the other side, the people we are talking to may be unsure whether or not we will accept them with their new beliefs. They are often afraid of being rejected, accompanied with feelings of loss, anger, and sadness. Yet despite these difficulties and barriers, with awareness we can almost always find positive ways to relate to those who are undergoing a faith transition; we can find ways to set aside our different viewpoints and fears and set a positive tone by reassuring them of our acceptance and showing them love and compassion.

Validating

Validation is showing others, both during and after listening, that we accept and respect them and their feelings and experiences. The psychologist Karyn Hall offers an insightful definition of validation:

> Validation doesn't mean agreeing or approving. When your best friend or a family member decides something you really don't think is wise, validation is a way of supporting them and strengthening the relationship while maintaining a different opinion. Validation is a way of communicating that the relationship is important and solid even when you disagree.[30]

For example, when talking with a friend about why they no longer attend church, they express concerns about early Church history and say they do not believe Joseph Smith was a prophet, or perhaps more severely, they say that they believe he was a fraud. What do we do? We have had spiritual experiences that lead us to believe that Joseph was a prophet, that he translated the Book of Mormon through the power of God, and that he saw Father in Heaven and Jesus Christ in a grove of trees. We feel this deeply. Do we stay silent? Do we tell the other person about our experiences? Do we testify? If our purpose is to build a strong relationship, our best response is to validate them by accepting the reality of their feelings. Validating includes showing that we are listening, that we won't turn away, and that we are trying to understand how they feel. This validation can be communicated through such statements as:

- Thank you for explaining.
- I can see how hard this is for you.
- Tell me more.
- When did you start feeling this way?
- Okay.
- I see.

As I have learned and studied the principles of listening, avoiding harmful interactions, and building positive relationships, I have felt my own relationships being blessed as they became more authentic and meaningful. For instance, I have learned from the women in my life how women often see issues regarding the Church differently than I do. They have taught me how valuable their perspective is, and I am more inclined to ask them their opinion because they have valuable insights that I wouldn't get by talking to only men. I have also become aware of generational differences and have greater respect for millennials. Whether learning from someone of a different culture, race, or life experience, I have become humbler as I grow increasingly aware of how much I can learn from others. I have also seen the healing that can come just by listening. I so wish I had known and practiced these principles before now, but I am grateful that I can build upon this understanding from now on. There is always more we can do to listen, understand, and build meaningful relationships based on Christlike attributes. It's a lifelong pursuit. As we faithfully show gentleness, meekness, love unfeigned, kindness, and, throughout it all, an increase in love, our relationships will grow stronger than the cords of death. It doesn't happen all at once, but over time it distills upon us as the dews from heaven (D&C 121:41–45).

CHAPTER 10

Ministering at Church

*Our opportunity as covenant-keeping daughters [and sons] of God is
not just to learn from our own challenges; it is to unite in empathy and
compassion as we support other members of the family of God in their
struggles, as we have covenanted to do.*

—Carole M. Stephens[1]

This chapter discusses specific ways we can create trust, belonging,
and meaning for those who question their belief or participation in the
Church. This includes what ward leaders can do to create a culture that is
more welcoming, inclusive, and faith-promoting to those with doubts. I
also review what we as Church members can do to support these objectives. If you are a ward leader, I hope this chapter will give insight into
ways you can lead your ward or organization to address today's concerns
of faith. Better understanding these issues will help direct our prayers and
identify areas where we need guidance. If you are not a leader, I hope the
suggestions outlined in this charter will inspire you to find ways to create a culture that supports those who want to worship but feel they are
unwelcome or don't belong.

An Invisible Problem

It's not always apparent when someone has questions or doubts. From
the outside, a person may appear to be a fully believing member of the
Church, when in reality they are struggling with their testimony or desire
to participate. The person may be unwilling to trust others with their
questions, doubts, and true beliefs. In the introduction to this book, I
mentioned a bishop who thanked a stalwart couple for their service only
to discover they had significant doubts and had decided to no longer attend church. The bishop hadn't recognized their struggles before, and it
was now too late for him to address their concerns.

Though the couple had announced their decision that day, it had really been months and years in the making. Looking at the *Faith Crisis
Member Survey*, 78 percent of respondents agreed that "from the outside
they appeared as a traditionally believing member of the Church." These
people are struggling inside, but no one knows it. And this sentiment does

not just apply to lay Church members who identify as being in a faith crisis. In the *Local Leader Survey*, I asked local Church leaders about their belief, and I was surprised at how many expressed doubt and concern, at how they viewed judgment at church, and how only a minority felt strongly that they fit in.

Rate Each Statement
(Local Leader Survey)

	Strongly Agree	Agree
There are some teachings of the Church that are troubling to me or difficult for me to believe.	10%	30%
While as an adult member, I have had times with significant doubt.	14%	26%
Sometimes I feel a culture of judgment at church.	25%	53%
I feel like I fit in.	30%	51%

When we go to church, it's easy to look around, see everyone in their Sunday best, and believe that all is well. Some, however, are more like a duck in a pond—they look like all is well on the surface of the water, but underneath and invisible to onlookers, their legs are furiously kicking to stay on course. We keep doubts and concerns to ourselves mostly because we want to belong.

I remember talking with one bishop about faith challenges in his ward, and he confidently said that he did not see the importance of addressing faith challenges with his congregants because they were highly active and did not have those concerns. He may have been right, but if the data from the surveys are even marginally representative of his ward, the issues are there, perhaps lying just below the surface. If left unaddressed, he may have an experience like other bishops who discovered it was too late to address the faith concerns of previously believing and contributing Church members.

Not being able to see the faith struggles of individuals may explain why these challenges are not often discussed in our wards. In previous chapters, I presented data that show most local Church leaders believe addressing issues related to faith crises is important. (Sixty-five percent of local leaders strongly agreed that it was very important to address these issues in their ward; only 2 percent said it was unimportant.) Yet most leaders indicated that faith challenges were not being addressed sufficiently in their wards.

How Has Your Ward Addressed Faith Challenges?
(*Local Leader Survey*)

	Agree
Introduced the Gospel Topics Essays.	10%
Held special sacrament meeting talks.	17%
Through the fifth Sunday lessons.	26%
Created separate Sunday School class on difficult topics.	3%
Created specialized calling to support leaders.	3%
Discussed in Relief Society or Elders Quorum first Sunday council meetings.	24%
Through special lessons in Sunday School or third-hour meetings.	9%
Focused discussions in ward council.	30%
Not addressed.	54%

Despite many possible avenues for addressing issues related to faith crises at church, the data indicate that they are being discussed only rarely. Seventy percent of participants indicated that faith challenges weren't discussed in their ward councils—perhaps the most obvious place for such discussions. Fifty-four percent indicated that these issues weren't addressed at all in their wards. If issues related to faith crises are universally thought of as important, why are they not addressed more directly? Perhaps leadership is overwhelmed with other urgent issues and finds it difficult to focus on problems that are challenging to address. Without experience or training, we likely don't have ready solutions or approaches to these issues. In both surveys, I asked participants to rank their level of agreement with the statement "Discussing challenging history, doctrine, or policy creates more problems than it solves." Only 25 percent of leaders either agreed or strongly agreed. Those in the *Faith Crisis Member Survey* responded similarly, with only 22 percent strongly agreeing or agreeing. So while some may see merit in avoiding difficult issues, a strong majority apparently do not.

Making Church a Place of Ministering

For many of us, our Sunday meetings and classes are places where we gather together to minister and be ministered to. We trust in the Church and its leaders, find belonging with other Saints, and seek answers to spiritual questions and guidance for our lives. However, some do not fully feel that sense of trust, joy, and belonging—sometimes because of concerns about general Church leaders but often because of what they experience and feel when they attend and socialize with the Church community. Regardless of whether or not we have a leadership calling, each of us helps determine whether church is a place of trust, belonging, and meaning.

I'm not suggesting that church should be anything other than a place where we can learn about living Christlike lives and find hope in the promises our Heavenly Parents have made to us. It should be a place where we can feel the love of the Savior, not a place of contention where every controversial idea is discussed and debated. However, it should also include space for all to worship and participate in ways that make it feel like home. The other day I talked with a man named Jim who stopped believing and attending church several decades ago. As we discussed the average church experience, he said, "It's Sydney or the bush"—an Australian saying that means "it's all or nothing." In other words, he was expressing common sentiment that there isn't a way for someone to participate in the Church if they are not a complete believer.

When Jim stopped attending, he believed in Christ and wanted to live his life in a Christlike way, but he did not believe that the Church had a monopoly on truth. He found it difficult to participate because he didn't agree with the claim that The Church of Jesus Christ of Latter-day Saints is the only true and living church. We spent about an hour talking about whether someone like him could find space at church, even though we do teach and believe that the Church has a unique role within the Plan of Salvation. Is there a place in our wards for Jim or for others who don't fully believe in every doctrine?

Being Welcoming and Inclusive

Church leaders have been clear that we should welcome all who want to worship with us. In an October 2014 General Conference address, Elder Dieter F. Uchtdorf urged Latter-day Saints to be more inclusive of everyone of varying levels of belief:

> The Church of Jesus Christ of Latter-day Saints is a place for people with all kinds of testimonies. There are some members of the Church whose testimony is sure and burns brightly within them. Others are still striving to know for themselves. The Church is a home for all to come together, regardless of the depth or the height of our testimony. I know of no sign on the doors of our meetinghouses that says, "Your testimony must be this tall to enter."[2]

This is not some new idea. Over a century ago President Joseph F. Smith expressed a very similar sentiment:

Members of the Mormon church are not all united on every principle. . . . But so long as a man believes in God and has a little faith in the Church organization, we nurture and aid that person to continue faithfully as a member of the Church though he may not believe all that is revealed.[3]

We have also been told that we become a better people when we include everyone. A year earlier in another General Conference address, Elder Uchtdorf stated,

To those who have separated themselves from the Church, I say, my dear friends, there is yet a place for you here. Come and add your talents, gifts, and energies to ours. We will all become better as a result.[4]

I personally feel that I become a better person when I listen to the experiences of people whose lives are different than mine. I learned of the scars of war when I served as the home teacher of a man who had served in World War II. He had liberated a Jewish concentration camp fifty years earlier, and in the twilight of his life, he suffered as he remembered the horrific scenes of the Holocaust. I also learned about faith from a man who had always served and participated in church but couldn't firmly say he had ever had a spiritual experience. His wife had a sure testimony of the gospel, but he did not. Nevertheless, he still carried on with hope and a small amount of faith.

Diversity among Church members is not just permissible, it is necessary for our wards to reach their full potential. Speaking on this subject, Elder Jeffrey R. Holland encouraged those who have questions and doubts to value their individuality and to continue participating in the Church:

Remember it is by divine design that not all the voices in God's choir are the same. It takes variety—sopranos and altos, baritones and basses—to make rich music. To borrow a line quoted in the cheery correspondence of two remarkable Latter-day Saint women, "All God's critters got a place in the choir.". . . Now, this is not to say that everyone in this divine chorus can simply start shouting his or her own personal oratorio! Diversity is not cacophony, and choirs do require discipline . . . but once we have accepted divinely revealed lyrics and harmonious orchestration composed before the world was, then our Heavenly Father delights to have us sing in our own voice, not someone else's.[5]

We are better people when we worship and learn from those who are different than us. I am not a great singer, but last year I joined the ward choir. I can't sing anything higher than a middle C, and even that note I can't sing reliably. With high notes, I usually fake it and just mouth the words. But when the music goes an octave below, I am confident and reliable in singing the notes, and I feel the music with my full heart. If I'm having trouble singing something, I sometimes raise my hand and ask the director for guidance. Other times she already knows we don't know the music well enough yet, and she has us practice it repeatedly until I can handle the rhythm and find my note while other parts are singing theirs. I admit there are times when I know that no amount of practice is going to help me get it and that we should just move on. In those moments, I remain silent and try to not sabotage others when we perform. I find joy in music and am grateful the director and my fellow choir members let me participate. Hymns help me feel closer to Christ, and I enjoy being with other people and establishing relationships outside of a class or lesson. I am not perfect, but they welcome me anyway and value my contribution, meager as it may be. They make me feel and know that I belong.

We can likewise make sure that those who don't believe everything taught at church are welcomed and embraced. We do this when we open our arms to an investigator who has limited understanding of our beliefs; we can open our arms in the same way to sincere members who have doubts or questions. Joan was an example of this when bearing her testimony in sacrament meeting. Based on this woman's constant service and participation, I know she was a faithful and believing member of the Church. In her testimony she described how the temple was difficult for her as a woman. She was honest and vulnerable in her remarks. She described how she was working through her feelings and concerns. I think she mentioned her struggles in order to share with others in a positive way that even she, a constant and faithful sister, had concerns. She described how she dealt with those concerns and continued to participate even though her questions were left unresolved. Through her example, she gave permission for people to have concerns and share them, and she patterned how to do so in a faithful and believing way. Being open and honest can be hard to do, however, when we feel pressure to play the role of a perfect Church member or when we don't feel comfortable sharing those parts of our lives that don't meet some ideal standard. Although Joan's concerns were likely addressed with recent changes in the temple ceremonies, I admire her vulnerability in admitting her challenges with faith. Like Joan, as Church leaders and members, we can help make people feel more comfortable by reaching out to those who are different from us and by sharing our own vulnerabilities.

Being Inclusive in Church Classes

In George Orwell's classic *1984*, a taskforce of secret police is charged with uncovering and punishing "thoughtcrime," which is expressing information and viewpoints that go against official teachings or are socially unacceptable. Winston, the main character of the book, copes with a society that punishes those who believe differently than the established position. Unfortunately, things do not end well for him. While we obviously do not criminalize "thoughtcrime" at church in the same manner, we do sometimes reprimand those who think differently. I'm sure we've all been in a Gospel Doctrine class when someone said something a little unorthodox and their comment was policed or testified against.

Policing isn't simply stating a different opinion. It occurs when someone wishes to not just correct but stop someone they disagree with or believe to be in error. Over the course of the last year, I have seen this kind of policing occur more than once in classes in my own ward and in others I have visited. For example, in one Gospel Doctrine class someone shared their view that the story of Job was likely an allegory; another responded by strongly testifying that Job was an actual person. This response wasn't given as someone offering a different opinion, but rather as divinely sanctioned declaration that the other person was wrong. I witnessed a similar interaction when the topic was the story of the global flood. Likewise, my wife once expressed in a Sunday class that she thinks we have too many battle hymns, and she was given an earful from those who think singing about war is an important part of the restored gospel. In each of these examples the underlying message was clear: only views deemed permissible or correct by the responders were allowed in church meetings.

I hope that no one was hurt in these exchanges, but as I talked with the *Faith Crisis Member Focus Group* I discovered that most of the participants have felt policed at church, which has caused them to feel that they can't authentically participate. When someone else gets reprimanded in class, it signals to others that if they raise an alternative view or have a question that is considered askew, they will be looked at differently or even verbally attacked. Even if only one person makes a harsh comment, every class member learns the cost of violating the assumed boundaries and the whole group is policed.

How we teach and participate in our classes largely determines whether people feel they authentically belong at church. Brené Brown asked middle school students about the key to learning, and she summarized their response:

> There are times when you can ask questions or challenge ideas, but if you've got a teacher that doesn't like that or the kids in the class make fun of people who do that, it's bad. I think most of us learn that it's best to just keep your head down, your mouth shut, and your grades high.[6]

We can't learn if we don't feel comfortable sharing our concerns. I have similarly experienced times in classes at church when I realized my comment wouldn't be welcome, and I knew it was better to go along with what was being said rather than raise my hand with a question, concern, or different viewpoint. I also recognize times when I have policed others in the past, and I am working to be more affirming.

What can we do to create a supportive and welcoming classroom environment for those who have questions or concerns or just feel disconnected from Church culture? First, we need to learn to see policing when it happens. If we look around us during our classes, we'll notice it. It's a rare ward in which policing doesn't occur in some way. We might see it as overtly as in the examples I have illustrated, or it might appear more subtly in a person's tone of voice or in dismissive or judgmental body language. It can also happen when a comment is greeted with silence.

Second, we can find ways to affirm the comments given in class that we think might be policed. If we are teachers, we can vocally affirm a comment as soon as it's given. We can say, "I'm glad you brought that up. I can see how one could feel that." Or, "That is a really interesting idea. I am going to think about it. Thank you for sharing." Or, "I have never thought about it like that. I'm so glad we can look at things with different perspectives." If we are students, we can simply turn and look at the person who is speaking and show our interest through a nod. When we do wish to counter someone else's comment, we can do so gently by identifying our statement as an opinion and to phrase it in terms that don't come off as correcting the other person. We can soften our comment by saying, "I don't think we know for sure, but I have always felt that Job is a real person." Or, "It may just be me, but I really enjoy some of the war songs, but I see your point." The issues we disagree on are almost always things for which we don't really have clear answers, and even if we think we do, it's more helpful and productive to create space for someone who believes differently than it is to shut them down. In the classroom, whether as teachers or students, we should imagine ourselves putting away our sheriff's badge and think of ourselves as ministers.

Third, we can teach our ward members and teachers how to respond when someone makes a comment or asks a question that seems to go against the status quo. This instruction could be given in a sacrament meeting talk, in a discussion led by a teacher before starting a lesson, or in a teacher council meeting. Policing usually disappears when we become aware of it, and teaching others about it is something even people without a formal leadership calling can do. For example, as students we can model this behavior through our own affirming comments, particularly if another class member has already made a policing comment and we want to find a way to make the person who made the original comment feel supported. We can say things like, "I know some people feel differently, but I have always felt that Job is an allegorical story. I find it concerning that God and Satan would plot about Job's experiences. Thinking about it allegorically allows me to apply its principles without worrying about those issues." And as I have already suggested, we can find ways to affirm someone if they don't agree with established Church positions or general doctrines by saying things like, "I know there are some that don't agree with the Church's position. I am grateful you feel comfortable enough with us to express your feelings." Comments like this demonstrate to others helpful ways of responding, and they send a message to those who make unorthodox comments that we accept them and value their participation.

Do we tolerate questions? Or are we policing our borders of behavior and belief? President M. Russell Ballard taught seminary and institute teachers that we should value honest questions and engage with those who have those questions:

> We have heard stories where someone asking honest questions about our history, doctrine, or practice were treated as though they were faithless. This is not the Lord's way. . . . We need to do better in responding to honest questions. Although we may not be able to answer every question about the cosmos or about our history, practices, or doctrine, we can provide many answers to those who are sincere.[7]

Some may wonder what to do when someone "start[s] shouting his or her own personal oratorio." If someone comes across as too forceful in their opinions or contrary beliefs, it may be a sign that the person doesn't feel we will hear their sincere concerns unless they are expressed ardently.

When our culture silences sincere voices, some people's response will be to speak louder. We can, however, change the culture in our ward, Sunday School classes, and seminary and institute classes. We should first be patient and expand our borders of tolerance. We should also have humility concerning our own views of the gospel and interpretations of scripture. In an April 8, 1843, sermon, the Prophet Joseph Smith pointed to our lack of creeds fixing our doctrine and how that gives us freedom to have different beliefs. He was particularly critical of members attempting to police a brother for supposed false doctrines:

> I did not like the old man being called up for erring in doctrine. It looks too much like the Methodist, and not like the Latter-day Saints. Methodists have creeds which a man must believe or be asked out of their church. I want the liberty of thinking and believing as I please. It feels so good not to be trampled. It doesn't prove that a man is not a good man because he errs in doctrine.[8]

At times when contention arises or when people begin arguing against what we believe to be core doctrines, a teacher or someone who has rapport with the individuals involved can privately talk with them and minister to them by listening, understanding, and validating the sincerity of their concerns. In extreme and unusual circumstances, the bishop or another can meet with them and listen to their concerns and try to understand the reasons for their forceful arguments. If their anger is a result of not feeling heard, through listening, we may be able to allay their concern, or we may be able to find another way in which the concern can be discussed. We can explain the importance of letting others participate in a way that gives them peace and hope.

Finding Faithful Ways to Address Concerns

For those who have questions or worries about the Church, it can be hard to find faithful ways to resolve or even discuss their concerns. For example, if someone was concerned about the origins of the Book of Abraham, where would they go? The topic is not covered in the Church's curriculum (at least at the time of the writing of this book). Even if it were, at church we study the Pearl of Great Price only once every four years, so the person might have to wait years before the topic was covered in class. Further, a single Sunday School or seminary or institute class would likely not be able to sufficiently cover or resolve the issue.

There must be other, faithful avenues for people to discuss challenging issues with other Latter-day Saints who know about the topics. If we don't establish church as an open and safe place for these conversations, those with questions will turn to people outside of the Church or search for answers on the internet. We leave them on their own to seek answers wherever they can find them. Though sometimes they will find good answers, often the answers they find will lack a faithful perspective. If we don't help them, they may lose trust that the Church and its leadership can answer the questions that are important to them. Many faith-challenging issues don't have clear answers; we simply don't know enough, so in addition to communicating the best information we have, we may need to help others see a pathway of faith even in the absence of straightforward answers.

So what can we do? One faithful source of information the Church has created are the Gospel Topics Essays, which the Church has published and translated into multiple languages on its website. They provide background on topics that are troubling for some, including the origins of the Book of Abraham, polygamy, Mountain Meadows Massacre, the Book of Mormon translation, and priesthood. The essays provide reliable history and context, but they haven't been widely introduced and are relatively unknown among most Church members. Those of us who know about the essays can make efforts to introduce them to others. One sister, for example, saw a need for the Gospel Topics Essays to be addressed in her ward, and she discussed that need with the bishop. The bishop, after consulting with the stake president and getting his approval, asked the woman to teach from the essays once a month in Gospel Doctrine class. The first class introduced the essays and the class's plan for studying them—each month they would read one essay from start to finish. Because the class was short, they didn't have time to discuss the essays in detail, but each member in the ward became familiar with them as a resource. Although this approach would not work in the new two-hour block, it illustrates how one bishop saw a need and found a way to address it.

I talked with this sister about the class, and she reported that the essays were very well-received. She felt that even for those who didn't have any concerns, studying the essays helped them learn of the Church's efforts to be transparent with its history and provided them with materials to help those with questions about specific issues. She encouraged those with concerns to study the footnotes for additional information and sources. I am sure there were people in the class who had concerns and who, as a result of the class, felt more trust in the ward and its efforts to address difficult issues and help build faith. Parents in the class also gained information and resources that could help them better teach their children if their children develop concerns about the topics addressed in the essays. The class also may have helped those who felt they couldn't address controversial issues at church and perhaps made them feel more comfortable being authentic with their concerns.

A similar class could be offered in other wards. Perhaps a bishop could call a special Gospel Doctrine teacher who could organize and lead ad-hoc classes to address questions. The teacher's role could be widely announced in the ward, and then when a member had a question or a leader became aware of someone who had a concern, they could use this teacher to create a setting where the issue could be discussed.

My stake created a Tuesday night institute class to address faith-challenging issues. People could attend as they wanted, and the teacher would address specific concerns that the class members had. They covered a wide range of historical and contemporary issues. They would meet, open with a prayer, discuss the issue at hand, and share additional resources. Most issues are complex and don't have clear-cut explanations, but people in the class would suggest ways of thinking about these issues that both validated people's concerns and maintained a faithful perspective. For some people, the class was very helpful and allowed them to voice concerns that couldn't be effectively handled in a regular meeting like Sunday School. The key to the success of this class was having a mature teacher who could lead the class and moderate it in a way that ensured a positive tone. This type of weekday meeting could be implemented in almost any ward or stake. Or, with the new emphasis on family, home, and group study, individuals could meet as needed in a small home-based group on Sundays to discuss certain issues. To try and ensure positive and thoughtful discussions, teachers could ask participants to come spiritually prepared, perhaps even fasting, in order to invite the Spirit into the class.

As I discussed in Chapter 5, someone who has had a faith crisis will likely never be able to believe as they did previously. They need to see a pathway forward that still allows them to find hope, faith, and belief, even as they think about their faith differently. To find this pathway, a mentor who has had similar experiences and still has found a way to stay in the Church can be helpful. Together they can find a way to come unto Christ within a new faith framework. Church leaders can help create these mentorships and provide a faithful environment for members who are experiencing a faith crisis through ministering assignments. We can formally assign a mentor to listen, understand, and minister to another member who may be struggling, and once a relationship is created, that mentor can discuss and model a way to move forward in faith.

In a ward we have many leaders, including Relief Society, Sunday School, and Elders Quorum presidents, who are called and set apart to strengthen the faith of adults in the ward. Each can receive revelation on how to address today's concerns of faith and can also counsel together with other ward leaders to determine ways to address them. In the examples I have given, local leaders saw needs and did their best to address them through innovative approaches. Even members who don't have leadership callings can counsel with their leaders and give them ideas on ways to address these issues. I believe that with our best thinking and the Lord's guidance, we can find solutions that meet the unique needs of our congregations and members.

Reconsidering the Concept of Worthiness

At church we use the term "worthiness" to define the behaviors and beliefs we must have to be in harmony with the basic tenants of the gospel. If we are considered worthy, we can be granted permission to enter the temple, participate in ordinances, and receive certain callings. Our doctrines encourage us to continue to strive to be worthier and more valiant in our quest to become Christlike. Outside of the Church, worthiness means something different. The *Merriam-Webster* dictionary defines "worthy" first as "having worth or value"; its second definition is "having sufficient worth or importance."[9] Although "worthiness" comes from the word "worth," which I define as moral or personal value, being worthy to enter the temple or qualify for exaltation is completely different than having worth or value before God or others. Unfortunately, we as Church members sometimes confuse the concept of having inherent worth with the concept of ecclesiastical worthiness.

A word related to "worth" is "shame." When we feel that we are not worthy or do not have worth, we sometimes experience shame. Brené Brown defines shame as "the intensely painful feeling or experience of believing that we are flawed and therefore unworthy of love and belonging—something we've experienced, done, or failed to do makes us unworthy of connection."[10] Brown contrasts shame with guilt:

> Shame is a focus on self. Guilt is a focus on behavior. Shame is, "I am bad." Guilt is, "I did something bad." How many of you, if you did something that was hurtful to me, would be willing to say, "I'm sorry. I made a mistake"? How many of you would be willing to say that? Guilt: I'm sorry. I made a mistake. Shame: I'm sorry. I am a mistake.[11]

Guilt can help us recognize when we have fallen short and motivate us to be better; shame, on the other hand, causes us to feel unvalued, which makes it difficult for persons to get away from unhealthy behavior.

Sometimes our emphasis on doing all we can to be worthy in the eyes of God causes us to feel that we don't measure up, that we are not worthy of love, or that we can't belong to a community of Latter-day Saints who we think are living to a higher standard. A friend once shared with me something that his psychologist told him: "You Mormons never feel your work is done. It's like there is an ever-receding horizon of what is expected of you." As we stretch to try and reach the ever-receding horizon, sometimes we do so in ways that are righteous and positive, but at other times we become oppressive with a toxic focus on perfectionism. Perfectionism is a constant focus on the gap between our current selves and some ideal version of ourselves. Since we are imperfect beings, attaining perfection is impossible—we can never do enough. For some, as they try to reach perfection, they run beyond their strength and neglect their own mental and physical health or the needs of others. They define themselves by what they are not doing and, in the process, feel they never can be enough. They feel shame for their inadequacies and may feel that those around them, or even God, won't love and accept them. The ever-receding horizon becomes a curse, and they feel they don't belong.

It's not just the perfectionist or the fully active and believing Church member who is worthy in God's eyes, but also those who don't have full belief or even those who aren't keeping all the commandments. No one should ever feel that they don't have worth or that they aren't worthy of our love. We believe that "the worth of souls is great in the sight of God" (D&C 18:10). Each soul. Full stop. No exceptions. In fact, this love that God has for all is the perfection that Jesus said we ought to emulate in his Sermon on the Mount. Taken out of context, Jesus's declaration to "Be ye therefore perfect, even as your Father which is in heaven is perfect" (Matt. 5:48) is often mistaken to being a command to live a sinless life—leaving many to wonder how such a requirement could be possible. Read in context of the preceding verses, it becomes clear that the perfection Jesus spoke of here is the perfect (complete) love of God who "maketh his sun to rise on the evil and on the good, and sendeth rain on the just and on the unjust" (v. 45). Imperfect or incomplete love would be one that excluded some, whereas perfect love is universal and given to all. Elder Uchtdorf beautifully spoke of the universality of God's love for everyone when he said,

> Though we are incomplete, God loves us completely. Though we are imperfect, He loves us perfectly. Though we may feel lost and without compass, God's love encompasses us completely. He loves us because He is filled with an infinite measure of holy, pure, and indescribable love. We are important to God not because of our résumé but because we are His children. He loves every one of us, even those who are flawed, rejected, awkward, sorrowful, or

broken. God's love is so great that He loves even the proud, the selfish, the arrogant, and the wicked.[12]

Regardless of our actions, we are all loved by our perfect Heavenly Parents and the Savior. We are of worth to them. We should always remember that they love us, no matter. Similarly, regardless of our behaviors or status in the Church, we should never feel personal shame or that we are unworthy of connection and love—both from God and from those in our wards and families. Nor should we believe that others are unworthy of that same love. Sometimes we lack sensitivity and, whether inadvertently or on purpose, we dismiss or diminish others because we don't think they have enough faith or keep enough of the commandments. We may even dismiss them because we judge them to be one of the elect who are deceived (Matt. 24:24) or that they are a tare that will be burned at the last day (Matt. 13:25–30). Some may feel it's a waste of time to focus on these "tares" or the "deceived elect" or believe that people only have worth if they are willing to consider coming back to church. This is falsehood—people's worth is intrinsic. We cannot take it away.

Understanding the principle of inherent worthiness will make us more effective in our ministering since it will allow us to confidently testify of the importance of each soul. We can clearly communicate to others that they are important to us and to God no matter what they believe. No matter what they do, we love them. We can express this love in our classes and sacrament meeting talks, in our council meetings, and when we personally bear our testimonies. When we really feel and believe that everyone is worthy of love and connection, that belief will guide our actions to reflect more love and patience.

Disassociating Worth from Leadership Callings

Unlike many denominations, we call all our local leaders out of our congregations. Several of us start serving at a young age in youth quorum and class presidencies. We rightfully respect our leaders, and we recognize the authority and sacred callings of our bishops and stake presidents. But sometimes that awareness and respect can turn into status-seeking. I recall being a deacon and becoming aware of the status that comes from serving in a leadership position: When I was only twelve years old, I would pay close attention each time the deacons quorum presidency was reorganized. Simply being the deacons quorum president caused me to see them differently—as someone more capable and righteous than others in our quorum. When I was thirteen, I wondered if I would be called to be the deacons quorum president. I remember a sense of pride when I was. I'm naturally a prideful person, so maybe this reaction was unique to me. But perhaps I also learned to value and seek after the status that comes with leadership from the Church culture I lived in. Since callings are considered callings from God, it's not a far jump to believe that those who have the most responsibility are those most favored by God.

This awareness of status associated with Church leadership extended throughout my youth and into my mission. I recall being aware of how long someone was on their mission before they were called to be a district leader or zone leader. Such a calling was a badge of status and a marker of righteousness and future leadership potential. Though I remember being taught to avoid seeking for callings, that desire, at least for me, was hardwired. I doubt I am an exception. Our culture elevates those called to leadership positions as we acknowledge their words, give them special titles, recognize their presence, and thank them for their actions. Even though most Church members have been taught that callings don't define our worth, I have heard it said more than once that "it doesn't matter whether you serve as a bishop or in the nursery, it matters how you serve." But even in that saying, we imply status. I don't think we can completely avoid the status recognition that comes with leadership callings, but we can recognize it and find ways to minister in spite of it.

My brother Richard Ostler wrote about this topic in an article for *LDS Living*. He recounts, "I've been at meetings where the person speaking introduces himself by a list of his church callings." In so doing, they are letting us know that they are important and that their opinion is more important or valid than another's. Perhaps they do this because their past callings are tied to their own self-worth. Richard went on to say, "I've heard talks describing someone returning from inactivity and then state his calling ('he is now serving as the Bishop')." The message is that now that he is a bishop, his spiritual rescue is complete. Richard then talks about the impact this implication has on those who don't serve in leadership. He says,

> I've met with many outside of this leadership circle who feel deeply marginalized . . . feeling [they] are not part of this inner circle . . . not worthy . . . maybe their children not seeing them as equal to other fathers . . . their service in other Christlike ways not equally valued, appreciated or understood.[13]

In the *Faith Crisis Member Focus Group*, Joe told me he felt unworthy when a visiting authority described how stake presidencies are called. The visiting authority said that "[the Church authorities] go in and interview the top men in the stake." Upon hearing this, the man mentioned felt he did not have worth because he was not considered one of the "top men." At a different time, when a new stake president was called, the visiting authority said something similar about the twenty-six men he interviewed. These statements bothered the man, and he wrote a letter to the authority saying that he felt statements implied exclusivity. The authority sent a loving and humble response:

> I understand how the 'twenty-six men' comment could make one feel excluded and undervalued. In most stakes there are scores of men not interviewed who could successfully fulfill the calling of a stake president. We can certainly be wiser in the way we announce and sustain the brethren called so we can avoid any possible offense.[14]

Status is also sometimes awarded, whether intentionally or not, after leaders are released. Released leaders often continue to have credibility, for example, when they couch their opinions in their former leadership callings or their mission experiences. And some Church members will continue to refer to individuals in terms of their former callings years after they have been released, even referring to them with the titles of their past callings. It is also not uncommon to see members defer to past or present bishops or stake presidents as doctrinal or scriptural authorities (sometimes in an effort to police others). We may do this to build connection with the other person or to respect their past service, but it signals to some that, because they themselves did not hold a high calling in the past, they may not be as worthy or entitled to respect or that their views are somehow less valid.

When I was reading Richard's article to my wife, she astutely said, "Well, that's what it is like to be a woman"—rarely being considered to serve in presiding leadership roles or given the same opportunities at church to develop leadership qualities due to there being so few leadership roles available to women. Of course, some women may also feel pride when they are called to serve in the limited leadership callings available to them, such as Relief Society President. They may also feel pride when their husbands serve in leadership positions and perhaps a little let down when they don't.

God doesn't love leaders more than anyone else. They don't have more worth, even if they do happen to be great individuals who are spiritual, have leadership skills, or live a very Christlike life. By virtue of their callings, it's possible that they may even impact more lives than others do, but that doesn't mean God loves them more than any other person. Men who don't serve in leadership or who never are ordained a high priest have the same worth before God. Each soul is valued. Christ taught this when he recognized the contribution of a poor widow who gave her two mites. He said,

> Verily I say unto you, That this poor widow hath cast more in, than all they which have cast into the treasury: For all they did cast in of their abundance; but she of her want did cast in all that she had, even all her living. (Mark 12:43–44)

As this scripture illustrates, the highest contributions we can make in this life and to the kingdom of God have absolutely nothing to do with leadership or status within the Church. Each soul is precious.

Engaging Women and Listening to Their Perspectives

In 2017, my wife and I toured southern Europe. We attended church one Sunday in Italy and discovered it was ward conference. I didn't speak the language, so I mostly just watched the meeting and those participating. With a distracted mind, I looked at the stand and noticed that fifteen men and only one woman were visible to the congregation. The men included high counselors, the stake presidency, the bishopric, clerks, and the priests at the sacrament table. The woman sitting on the stand was the chorister who had no ecclesiastical authority and played a nonspeaking role. The meeting had no female speakers, although one woman did offer a prayer. I wondered what someone, particularly a woman, would think if this was her first time attending a Latter-day Saint meeting. Would she feel like she belongs? The optics were overwhelming. According to Jana Riess's research, 61 percent of millennials agreed that "women do not have enough say in the LDS Church."[15] I am sure that percentage is higher for millennial women.

Even the figures in our scriptures are overwhelmingly male. In the Book of Mormon, there are only four named women (and Mary the mother of Jesus is one of them). Almost all of our scriptural stories are about men, and when women do appear, they are often silent supporters like Lehi's wife Sariah. Due to our all-male priesthood, general conference talks are predominantly given by men. In Primary, most stories are about boys, and 85 percent of the pronouns in the Primary songbook are male. In our Sunday meetings, we generally have more male participation at the pulpit than female, where it is not uncommon to see only men giving talks and rare to see only women invited to offer them. Frequently when a couple speaks, the wife is asked to speak first and focus on introducing her family to the ward while the husband is asked to close the meeting by focusing on a doctrinal matter.

Women may struggle to belong in this overly male world. Church teachings highlight the eternal nature of gender, but we speak of exaltation as becoming like our Heavenly Father, something that half of our members cannot fully relate to. As a result, many women see their eternal destiny in Heavenly Mother and feel an unsatisfied desire to connect with her. Rachel Hunt Steenblik's poem, "What Every Child Wants to Know," embodies this desire:

> What every child wants to know is
> if her Mother is watching.
> What every child wants to know is
> if she is seen.[16]

While on our mission in Africa, my wife and I traveled to a different branch each Sunday. As the mission president, I was the presiding ecclesiastical leader in each branch we attended. On Sundays, my wife and I would meet with the branch presidency prior to sacrament meeting and ask them to observe when they felt the Spirit. Afterward, we would gather again and discuss their observations. I recall one time when a branch president said he had particularly felt the Spirit during the talks, which were all given by men. I asked why he thought he felt the Spirit, and he said the talks related to his life and the challenges he faced. I asked if he thought the women in the congregation felt the same about the talks. We discussed how women's experiences might be different than men's and how women can often relate better to talks given by other women. He got the point immediately, and from that time on, he involved more women in meetings. This point has stuck in my head. I regularly see ways in which women are treated as lesser participants in meetings. As mentioned, it remains disproportionately common for men to receive the respect and gravitas that comes with speaking last in sacrament meeting or for there to be more male than female speakers. Out of curiosity, I timed our last stake conference and found that out of one hundred minutes of speaking, only sixteen minutes were taken up by women. We need to do better.

The poet Henry Wordsworth Longfellow characterizes the feelings many have about how men can inadvertently treat women:

> . . . for it is the fate of a woman,
> Long to be patient and silent, to wait like a ghost that is speechless
> Hence is the inner life of so many suffering women
> Running through caverns of darkness, unheard, unseen, and unfruitful.[17]

The Church has made a lot of changes to address these issues. Elders and high priests have been combined into a single quorum, which decreased the gender imbalance in ward council and made the men's and women's organizations more parallel. Women's voices from early Church history are being highlighted in Church curriculum and the Church's new history, *Saints: The Story of the Church of Jesus Christ in the Latter Days.* Discourses from past female Church leaders were recently compiled and published by the Church in *At the Pulpit: 185 Years of Discourses by Latter-day Saint Women.*[18] These efforts have been well-received by Church members who value and want women's stories and experiences to be more available. We can do our part to bring these resources to light by incorporating them in our talks in church and in our comments in classes.

These efforts made by the Church are valuable not only because they help create more gender equality, which on its own is a worthy cause, but also because it brings more perspectives and life experiences into our worship. When we only hear from men or only read about men's experiences with God, we only get a part of the human experience and learn an incomplete and filtered gospel.

Women's lives are different than men's. Because of their virtual absence in scripture and in many discussions of today's challenges, women are often left without female role models or examples to learn from. We need women's voices—voices from today and yesterday—and we need to see the personal strength of women in their quest to become like their Heavenly Mother. It's not just women who need that; we as a people, both men and women, are better when we see and understand the experiences and heavenly potential of women and see examples of the feminine divine. In a short but poignant poem inspired by her son, Rachel Hunt Steenblick illustrates the yearning we all have:

What Søren Taught Me
Sons also
search for their
Mothers.[19]

We all need our mothers. I need my Mother.

After becoming aware of the gender imbalance in the world and in our Church culture, we should find ways to overtly address this imbalance. We are a church led primarily by men, but we need to ensure women are included at church and are able to fully participate in worship. Neylan McBaine identified many ways we can address these issues in our wards in her book *Women at Church: Magnifying LDS Women's Local Impact.*[20] We can do this by highlighting the issues and concerns of women, taking extra effort to find women's voices in scripture, conference talks, and history. We can also make sure we involve women in every way we can within the limits of current Church policy and doctrine. To overcome the shortcomings of our culture, our efforts to involve women need to be strong and clear. We can and should involve women more by making sure we quote them in our talks and lessons, call on them more in class lessons, go out of our way to give them leadership opportunities, and make sure we listen to their voices.

In the April 2014 General Conference, President Dallin H. Oaks gave a groundbreaking talk that expansively clarified how women participate in the priesthood. My wife and I were in Africa at the time the talk was given, living in a very patriarchal culture. Shortly after President Oaks's talk, we had a general authority visit for a conference. In the conference's leadership meeting, which included female leaders, he asked for a Relief Society president to stand up. One did. He then asked her if she had priesthood authority. She paused thoughtfully and then said she did. The general authority asked her why. She responded, "Because I have been set apart by someone with authority." She understood the power through which she served. In his talk, President Oaks said, "We are not accustomed to speaking of women having the authority of the priesthood in their church callings, but what other authority can it be?"[21] By understanding that women serve with priesthood authority and power, both because of their callings and also through their baptismal and temple covenants, we can better respect and revere their contributions accordingly.

With permission, I share the experience of an auxiliary president in a stake in the United States. Ashley's story demonstrates the need for us to include women in our decisions and to recognize their authority. During a recent stake council meeting, a discussion ensued about the schedule of a ward conference and how it would impact each organization in the stake. The meeting was conducted in the style of a lecture, not a council; everyone was told what had already been decided by the stake presidency. Then the discussion moved on to implementing changes associated with the newly announced two-hour block. Ashley had prepared for the council meeting by identifying issues she wanted to discuss with the council. As they were reading through the details of the changes, Ashley raised her hand and presented a few concerns she had. One of the counselors interrupted her and responded harshly that the stake presidency had already met and decided how each ward should do things, even though the strategies they were referring to were not proscribed by the Church. She pushed back, uncertain they fully understood her concerns. The stake president and counselor were visibly annoyed and patronizingly said that they just need to move forward and trust God.

I want to pause here and ask us to reflect on what we would do in this situation. I think stake councils are particularly difficult for women. The usual stake council has eighteen or so men and only three women. The overwhelming majority of men at the meeting can be daunting for a woman. Imagine being in Ashley's shoes—that we had prepared for the meeting and advocated our point of view and that we had been called and set apart and had the priesthood authority to help make a decision regarding the issue at hand—but instead of receiving the respect of having someone listen to our ideas, we get shut down and told that no one wants to hear from us. In this situation, many of us would probably defer to the power and authority of those men leading the meeting and would become silent and accept the status quo.

Ashley, like most of us would in this situation, felt vulnerable after speaking up and getting shut down. She knew if she said anything more, she would be seen as a disruptor. Ashley recounts,

> I could acquiesce, tone it down, hold back, and try to blend in. . . . My heart was beating, pounding through my chest all the way to my face. This felt wrong inside of me and I need to confront it, to understand it. Suddenly, the faces of all the capable, strong women I work with in this church came to my mind. The ways I have witnessed them seek and follow divine inspiration. Their faithful, humble desire to love and serve flowed into my heart and calmed the jitters in my intensity. This suddenly became a bigger deal. I had to speak for them.

She did. She spoke kindly, but sternly, saying,

> That's easy for you to say. You speak from a place of "authority" where you can have the final word and inspiration. But what about me? Do we get to lean into our own inspiration, trusting God? The truth is, the women have thought so much more about this than you have, and yet decisions are constantly being made without them. This is my specific responsibility and yet, if I say something different, I'm expected to yield my concerns or inspiration to you. It's hard to figure out what my role or purpose is if my voice never really has the same weighted value.

The moments following her comment were filled with tension and discomfort. She even saw one of the male leaders roll their eyes. They discussed the matter some more, and Ashley expressed love as they concluded the discussion. They moved on without a firm resolution on the issue. She was shaking and squeezed the hand of another female stake leader and steadied herself. A few minutes later, the stake president stopped before concluding the meeting and said, "I had the wrong approach earlier, and I am so grateful we could counsel together so I can improve and be better with others." The meeting ended, and Ashley received support from others as she walked to her car.

The next day, Ashley received a voicemail from the other counselor, who had sat silently throughout the exchange. He told her,

> I have not been able to stop thinking about that meeting and what you expressed. I found myself praying for you as you spoke, completely sympathetic to your concerns and hoping you could express them clearly . . . then cheering as you did.

Later that week her stake president met with her and told her he needed every word she shared. She felt his sincerity. They cried, they laughed, and Ashley said, "I felt the fullness of the gospel."

When I first heard this story, I was amazed. I have time and again seen Church leaders shut down comments from women in councils in similar ways, but I had never heard someone assert themselves in such an articulate yet forceful way. As I heard this story, I found myself, like the silent counselor, praying for it to resolve positively. I have seen similar situations resolve otherwise. Ashley was confident in her authority and her right to receive inspiration, and she saw the value she had in contributing to the discussion. Ashley's point was right; she has priesthood authority and is entitled to fulfill the responsibilities of her calling. She is a member of a council in which each person's opinion is valued. She has experience and understanding that others around the table need to hear and consider. She wasn't called to silently affirm; she was called to contribute her unique viewpoint and share the inspiration she has received while studying important issues. If we can create an environment where women's voices are heard and supported, without the risk and vulnerability that Ashley experienced, more women would make valuable contributions to our discussions. More women would participate. More women would feel like they belong. We would come a step closer to having women fully participate in church meetings and decision-making.

If Ashley had remained quiet, she may have left the meeting discouraged, perhaps becoming cynical. If her stake president hadn't responded the way he had, she may have left feeling defeated. In either of these alternative scenarios, what would the other female auxiliary presidents have learned about their roles? Ashley and the stake president patterned behavior that other Church members and leaders can learn from and follow; we can talk about difficult issues, create discomfort through honesty, and make better decisions at the end. The challenges of faith we have today requires engaging and hearing each voice in our councils.

Reflecting back on the meeting, I wonder what would have happened if the silent counselor had, instead of remaining silent, affirmed his support for Ashley in the meeting or if all those people who encouraged her in the parking lot had verbally supported her in the meeting. Perhaps her experience can inspire us to do better—we can be the ones who support future Ashleys, whose voices are being silenced. When we see something that devalues women in the Church, we need to say something and enable the voice that isn't being heard.

Using Our Councils

Inviting and listening to women's perspectives is one way our ward and stake councils can be more effective. These councils are key to addressing issues of faith because they require diverse perspective and organizational involvement. We need to go out of our way to support and make sure that everyone in our councils feels comfortable expressing their unique perspectives. Just as with women, the same is true for others who are not usually represented in Church leadership. When these individuals are not in our councils, we need to find them, ask them questions, and make sure their voices are heard. We can invite them to sit in on a council meeting to contribute to a discussion on a specific topic or ask a leader to meet with a group of people, listen to them, and report their thoughts back to the council. We need to prayerfully consider what kind of perspectives we need to include in our council meetings to make sure we truly understand the problems we are trying to solve and perhaps call those individuals to be council members.

We also need diversity in our councils to help ensure we see issues from all angles and meet the needs of everyone in our congregations. For example, if we are talking about the challenges that millennials face but everyone in the room is older than forty-five, we might not adequately understand those challenges as well as we could. If millennials are not already in the council, we could invite a group of them to attend a meeting, or we could even call someone to be a "millennial specialist," who would then be a formal member of the council and would attend meetings consistently. We could also have a member of the council meet with a group of millennials to discuss particular issues. When we take the time to seek out and understand the viewpoints of those ward members who are different than us, we will inevitably make better decisions. On the other hand, the inspiration we receive from God may be limited when we don't take the time to learn about challenges from those who are most familiar with them.

The instruction to use councils isn't new. In 1953 President Stephen L. Richards taught,

> The genius of our church government is government through councils. I have had enough experience to know the value of councils. Hardly a day passes but that I see . . . God's wisdom, in creating councils . . . to govern his Kingdom. . . . I have no hesitancy in giving you the assurance, if you will confer in council as you are expected to do, God will give you solutions to the problems that confront you.[22]

President M. Russell Ballard used this quote in two of his general conferences addresses and in his book *Counseling in Our Councils.*[23] Expanding on Richards's statement, Ballard says,

> Brethren, please be sure you are seeking the vital input of the sisters in your council meetings. . . . Ideally, all members of any Church or any family council should share their concerns and should suggest solutions based on gospel principles. I believe the Church and our families would be strengthened if stake presidents and bishops would use their council meetings for finding answers to [our most important] questions.[24]

Although I have never personally met Ashley, she has become one of my heroes. She bravely taught her stake council and all who have read her story about the importance of listening to women and other underrepresented voices.

The important questions that councils consider may differ across wards. One council might choose to discuss how to engage the ward's LGBTQ members and their families or to educate council members on the suicide risks of LGBTQ members. Another council may choose to consider how to teach our youth in ways that help them find meaning to life's most important questions. At other times, our councils might discuss how to create a less judgmental environment when we teach. Any issue I have addressed in this book will better be understood when it is discussed among several people with diverse viewpoints.

Ministering through Sacrament Meeting

Sacrament meetings may be our most powerful avenue for ministering. This is a time when the whole ward gathers together to participate in a sacred ordinance meant to connect us to Christ. As the meeting begins, we are usually greeted in a loving way. We sing hymns to remind us of our Savior, and as we partake of the sacrament we promise to take upon ourselves the name of Christ and follow his example. In return, we are promised redemption and forgiveness. We then get to hear from our members about their experiences of coming unto Christ. Through words spoken in sacrament meeting, we are often prompted to live our lives in a better way or to reach out to a person to whom we can minister. We always close the meeting in the name of Jesus Christ. Even though we hear only a few people speak, share, and testify during sacrament meeting, we can each have a personal experience as we try to connect with the speakers and apply their messages to our lives.

Handbook 2 instructs that in sacrament meeting, "talks and music should focus on gospel subjects that help members build faith and testimony."[25] As leaders choose sacrament meeting topics, and as we prepare and give talks, we can build faith by choosing to address issues related to trust, belonging, and meaning. If we are asked to give a talk, we can think about how to address the assigned topic in ways that will be considerate and inclusive of everyone. I could list hundreds of topics we could speak on and hundreds of ways we can help build trust, belonging, and meaning in sacrament meeting. In our council meetings, we ought to identify possible topics to address and potential speakers who would be uniquely able to speak to them. To get our minds thinking, here are examples of sacrament meeting topics that could help minister to those struggling with their faith:

- Learning to listen with empathy and love.
- Welcoming all our members.
- Understanding how we can sometimes be judgmental.
- Creating a culture of belonging.
- Understanding everyone is loved and valued by God.
- Ministering to those who question.
- Eliminating racism in our church, community, and lives.
- Standing for our values while loving and accepting people, even Church members, who have different values.
- Ministering to those with mental health challenges.
- Understanding why diversity strengthens us.

Some topics may be inappropriate or too complicated for a sacrament meeting and are better discussed in a fifth-Sunday lesson, including:

- Responding to the needs and challenges of LGBTQ members and their families, including addressing the high rates of suicide.

- Better accommodating persons with disabilities, autism, and other needs, and learning to better incorporate them in our classes, worship, and activities.

- Understanding unique generational concerns, particularly the concerns of millennials.

- Preventing and dealing with sexual abuse at church, in our homes, and in our communities.

- Understanding ways we feel shame and its impact on our relationship with God and in our wards and families.

- Learning about the Gospel Topics Essays and how to respond to challenges of Church history.

Of course, we do not need to be focusing on these kinds of issues every Sunday. Most of our talks and discussions should focus on and strengthen faith in all the usual ways. But in a measured way, we need to address the foundational concerns that are causing many to lose a sense of trust, belonging, and meaning at church.

We should thoughtfully select not only the topics we think our wards need to discuss, but also the speakers who will address them. Perhaps someone who is considered nontraditional in Church culture would be most effective in speaking about a certain topic in a faithful way. The message is more powerful when it comes from someone who has personal experience with the topic being considered, allowing them to be authentic in their remarks and increasing the likelihood that listeners will accept what they say. Speaking about faith challenges openly at church puts a stamp of approval on and normalizes discussing these issues without shame.

Sometimes at church when we say we "need people," we mean that we want to find ways to involve them at church so we can change them. But instead of trying to change them, we should recognize that because they have different experiences and beliefs, we need them to teach us about issues and challenges they face to help us develop understanding and empathy so we can become more Christlike. As they come to understand that we value their experiences and that they are essential to our understanding of faith and love, they will feel more belonging with us. And we, in turn, will become more edified; we will learn more about the human experience and gain insight that only they can provide. Truly, we need them and are richer when they participate.

Building Durable Faith in the First Place

Church is a place where we help people come unto Christ. It's a place where we can help those who are questioning their faith or who no longer believe. We can help them find ways to still trust the Church and its leaders, to feel they belong as their authentic selves, and to find meaning in Church doctrines and participation. As important as these efforts are, however, we should also find ways to prevent the disconnection and loss of faith some experience in the first place.

In so many ways, we already do this well. We learn from a young age the importance of keeping on the covenant path, of seeking the Spirit in our lives through prayer and study, and of seeing outside ourselves as we provide Christian service. But many of today's challenges are different than what we've experienced before, and thus we need to teach differently to better address these challenges. Speaking of these difficult issues, Bruce and Marie Hafen write, "In this day and age . . . we need to do a better job of introducing our children, young people, new converts, and others to the process of learning how to deal productively with complexity."[26] We need to prepare those around us for dealing with the complexity that almost all of us will face with today's challenges of faith. Terryl and Fiona Givens argue that we need tools, both as individuals and as congregations, to help us navigate today's faith challenges. Too often, however, "we want a script, and we find we stand before a blank canvas. We expect a road map, and we find we have only a compass."[27] To build faith that will be resilient in the face of challenges we need to learn and teach others how to live with the blank canvas or a simple compass—in other words, how to live with ambiguity and how to move forward with our faith, even though we may not always see where we are going. By doing so we will not only be able to build better bridges with those struggling with faith and better prepare ourselves and others for challenges, but we will also gain a more vibrant and expansive understanding of the gospel of Christ.

Summary

The many ways we can minister at church could fill a book or more. So much of whether or not someone maintains their faith is based on culture. With thoughtfulness, study, counseling, and listening, we can receive inspiration on how to create a culture in which everyone sincerely seeking feels welcome and belonging. In researching and interviewing for this book, I came to know Victor. I spent hours talking with him. He is in his fifties, and when I talked to him, he was in an active leadership calling. He has struggled with his testimony for all the reasons I have discussed—the Church's history, culture, doctrine, and policies. But he loves the Church and his ward community. He loves the people and considers us to be his "tribe." He wants to participate, and with the help and understanding of wise leaders, he has found a role that allows him to provide temporal service to people who really need it. He loves it. It gives him purpose, and he feels closer to Christ. His church service helps him connect to his believing family because he too can participate in church in a meaningful way. He isn't in Sydney the way most of us are, but he still managed to find faithful accommodation and doesn't have to live in the bush.

CONCLUSION

Not Walking Alone

Having compassion on those who are hurting for whatever reason and then translating the response of the heart into the needed act is truly ministering as God would have us do. . . . We must recognize that life is a precious gift, that trust and tenderness are fragile, that we must love and serve one another, must encourage one another—all this not once, but over and over again.

— Joy F. Evans[1]

When I had largely finished this book, I contacted Mike and Amanda (whose stories are in Chapter 1) to see how they were doing. Mike was a completely believing Church member who had been married in the temple and served a mission, but he lost his belief in the divinity of the Church about two years ago. Mike still believes in Christ and participates in church both for cultural reasons and because his wife is a believing member. Mike wrote me back just as I was getting ready to finalize this concluding section. Six months had passed since my initial interview with him, and when I read his words, I chose to replace what I had written with his remarks. He eloquently summarizes so many of the points in this book:

When I was in the dark night of the soul, there are a few things that could have really helped me.

I needed someone to just listen, and then after listening, let me know and help me really believe that they trusted me, and loved me no matter what conclusion I came to.

I needed someone to show me that it was love that was the strongest and largest cord that bound us together, not our common belief in the Church.

I needed someone to not only listen, but to encourage me to seek answers, to say: "Great! I don't know where this journey will take you, and it's your own journey, but whatever conclusion you come to, I will absolutely respect you. And if you want someone to walk with for a while on your journey, call me. I'm there for you."

I needed someone to let me know that they have never experienced what I'm experiencing, and so they would never pass judgment.

I needed to feel from people, not just hear words, that they trusted me and viewed me as a worthy, intelligent, and spiritually sensitive human being.

I needed a different space after sacrament meeting to be nourished spiritually, and if that wasn't available, I needed an invitation to leave during the rest of the church block to seek spiritual nourishment elsewhere. (I still need this.)

I needed someone to ask me, "What would you like to do in the ward that will help you thrive here?" For me that would have been teaching. I love to teach, but I became an "unsafe" person, and so I haven't taught since "coming out." I used to teach and speak frequently.

I also needed someone to listen and then push back a little. I needed someone with whom to engage in healthy confrontations, because after resolution of those confrontations, relationships can blossom.

I was lucky to have a wife, siblings, and parents who offered these things to me. It wasn't a walk in the park; rather it was the hardest thing we've ever done together. Those conversations were the hardest conversations we've ever had. The stretching, the anxiety, the frustration was agonizing. But we are now closer than we ever have been, and I wouldn't change ANYTHING.

If we could cultivate a culture at our meetinghouses and in our private homes that welcomes curiosity, investigation, vulnerability, honesty, realness, and freedom of thought, I would be much more interested in participating more in the Church. But right now, I have to hide part of myself, the deepest and most spiritual part of myself, for fear of discipline and social reprisal. So, I find that I'm slowly separating myself. Not being authentic, and not feeling like I'm allowed to be authentic, has proven to be a sure way to literally drive me to the brink of insanity. So, I stay distant, and don't fully engage, so I can be who I am, and believe what has taken me a lifetime of study, prayer, experience, and meditation to believe. I have a hope that our community will change. I have a hope that rather than basing relationships on shared beliefs regarding truth claims, we will base our relationships on love and authentically being a part of each other's lives. We all have so much to offer. Our individual stories are amazing, thrilling, terrifying, saddening, motivating, exhilarating, and so much more. If we are created in the image of God, and if God really is a part of us, then I love the scripture "This is eternal life, that they may know YOU. . . ." We get to know God by getting to know each other, and we can experience eternal life right here and right now if we let go of some old and dusty doctrines and policies that keep us from knowing the God within each of us. I hope our community will change to be a safer place for those of us who now find ourselves on the edge or on the outside.

This is the gospel. The love and understanding Mike outlines here are consistent with our teachings and with our handbooks. It is what we want for ourselves and for our family members, and it is the pathway of discipleship. It's the gospel of Jesus Christ.

Amanda also responded to my inquiry. She and her husband had stopped attending church about four months before I interviewed her. She stepped away because of an overwhelming anxiety stemming from the dissonance between what she heard in church and what she felt was true. Her feelings created tension with her family. In the six months since I interviewed her, she hasn't attended any church meetings. She still has church friends, and they don't pressure her to return. Instead they listen, understand, and express empathy. She still feels drawn to the Church community, but she doesn't want to participate in meetings. Our exclusive truth claims are difficult for her to accept given the good people around her, and she believes our exclusiveness negatively impacts her children. She told me,

> What I wish is that we Mormons could be content with being a good church, instead of insisting on being the one true church. I could keep my spiritual traditions and community without being disingenuous. I could honor the good within the Church and shun the bad, without being shunned. I understand why this is impossible with our current doctrine. We would have to give up some authority. We would have to apologize for our mistakes.

Amanda said that our simple interviews, where she felt listened to without judgment, were incredibly meaningful to her:

> It's hard to express how important it's been to be heard by you and others like you, who hold space in your hearts for uncomfortable realities and dissonant experiences and sorrows not your own. There are truths that have grown in prominence in my heart, and among those are empathy, peace with uncertainty, vulnerability, connection, courage, and love. Always love. Thank you for your courageous work and your big, open heart. I feel blessed to know you.

I'm grateful I could help. I heard this sentiment multiple times in my interviews: "Thanks for listening." "Thanks for asking." But they weren't the only ones who were helped. I sincerely believe I am a better person for knowing Amanda, Mike, and others like them. They have taught me and opened my eyes to see people in need and to know how to better reach them. Everyone, regardless of belief, should have people in their lives who they can share their most important, vulnerable, and meaningful thoughts, feelings, and beliefs.

This book isn't about happily ever afters. My comments here are meant to help us understand others and what they are facing so we can be more loving and make sure more people like Amanda or Mike feel comfortable worshipping with us with a more durable faith. I don't think Amanda will "come back" to the Church, and I am not sure Mike will "stay." In a way, that is beside the point. While our hearts and desires might be to help others return to being fully believing and participating Latter-day Saints, we must recognize that they might not ever return and choose to not let that get in the way of our relationships with them.

In the book *One Hundred Birds Taught Me to Fly,* Ashley Mae Hoiland writes about the difference between ministering to someone versus trying to save someone. Referring to an experience on her mission, she writes:

> We once left a home with a woman who spoke at us for hours without our even mentioning our purpose as missionaries. When we finally left, I, in frustration and anger, complained to my companion about what we were even doing out here in this uncared-for bit of desolation at the edge of a poor town listening to people talk nonsense for hours when we had the words that could save them. "No," my companion, a native to the country, said, "We are not here to save them. We are only here to minister to them." When I boarded a plane a year later to go home, I had not saved anyone. The thousands of lives I brushed up against left a mark on me, and I left a mark on some of them. My companion was right. We did not save. Through the grace of God we ministered with the kind of charity that grows between strangers, and more often than not, we were the ones ministered to.[2]

Those who question or leave the Church are precious children of our Heavenly Parents. They want us to love them, comfort them, and mourn with them, and we are blessed when we do. In our efforts to build a bridge of understanding, our families will have no empty chairs at the dinner table, our relationships will be more meaningful and our love richer, and our hearts will change as we better understand faith and learn to love more completely.

At its purest, the gospel plan is a bridge for us to return to our Heavenly Parents. Built on the Savior's Atonement, it is full of understanding, patience, and love. It's a pattern for us as through our earthly lives, we bless people and are blessed by them. With Christ as our example, we minster, listen to, understand, and are blessed by the Savior as he ministers to us and heals each of us on our own journey.

Recommended Resources

Academic Resources on Religious Retention and Disaffiliation

James W. Fowler, *Stages of Faith: The Psychology of Human Development and the Quest for Meaning* (New York: Harper Collins, 1981).

Robert P. Jones, Daniel Cox, Betsy Cooper, and Rachel Lienesch, *Exodus, Why Americans Are Leaving Religion—and Why They're Unlikely to Come Back* (Washington, DC: Public Religion Research Institute, 2016).

David Kinnaman and Aly Hawkins, *You Lost Me: Why Young Christians Are Leaving Church . . . and Rethinking Faith* (Grand Rapids: Baker Publishing Group: 2011).

Benjamin Knoll and Jana Riess, "'Infected with Doubt': An Empirical Overview of Belief and Non-Belief in Contemporary American Mormonism," *Dialogue: A Journal of Mormon Thought* 50, no. 3 (Fall 2017): 1–37. http://www.dialogue-journal.com/wp-content/uploads/sbi/articles/Dialogue_V50N03_12.pdf.

Pew Research Center, "2014 US Religious Landscape Study," http://www.pewforum.org/religious-landscape-study/.

Jana Riess, *The Next Mormons: How Millennials Are Changing the LDS Church* (New York: Oxford University Press, 2019).

Darren E. Sherkat, *Changing Faith: The Dynamics and Consequences of Americans' Shifting Religious Identities* (New York: NYU Press, 2014).

Robert Wuthnow, *Inventing American Religion: Polls, Surveys, and the Tenuous Quest for a Nation's Faith: Polls, Surveys, and the Tenuous Quest for a Nation's Faith* (New York City: Oxford University Press: 2013).

Faithful Resources Addressing Faith Given Today's Challenges

Terryl Givens and Fiona Givens, *The Crucible of Doubt: Reflections on the Quest of Faith* (Salt Lake City: Deseret Book, 2014).

Bruce C. Hafen and Marie K. Hafen, *Faith Is Not Blind* (Salt Lake City: Deseret Book, 2018).

Patrick Q. Mason, *Planted: Belief and Belonging in an Age of Doubt* (Salt Lake City: Deseret Book, 2015).

Patrick Q. Mason, "The Courage of Our Convictions: Embracing Mormonism in a Secular Age," (lecture, FairMormon Conference, 2016), http://www.fairmormon.org/conference/august-2016/courage-convictions.

Thomas McConkie, *Navigating Mormon Faith Crisis: A Simple Developmental Map* (Salt Lake City: Mormon Stages, 2015).

Adam S. Miller, *Letters to a Young Mormon*, 2nd ed. (Salt Lake City: Deseret Book, 2018).

Faithful Resources Addressing Church History and Contemporary Issues

M. Russell Ballard, "The Opportunities and Responsibilities of CES Teachers in the 21st Century," address to CES religious educators, Salt Lake Tabernacle, Salt Lake City, February 26, 2016, http://www.lds. org/broadcasts/article/evening-with-a-general-authority/2016/02/ the-opportunities-and-responsibilities-of-ces-teachers-in-the-21st-century.

Tom Christofferson, *That We May Be One: A Gay Mormon's Perspective on Faith and Family* (Salt Lake City: Deseret Book, 2017).

The Church of Jesus Christ of Latter-day Saints, "The Gospel Topics Essays," https://www.churchofjesuschrist.org/manual/gospel-topics-essays.

The Church of Jesus Christ of Latter-day Saints, "Church History Topics," https://www.churchofjesuschrist.org/study/history/topics.

Jane Clayson Johnson, *Silent Souls Weeping: Depression-Sharing Stories, Finding Hope* (Salt Lake City: Deseret Book, 2018).

Neylan McBaine, *Women at Church: Magnifying LDS Women's Local Impact* (Draper, UT: Greg Kofford Books, 2014).

Saints: The Story of the Church of Jesus Christ in the Latter Days, 4 vols. (Salt Lake City: The Church of Jesus Christ of Latter-Day Saints, 2018–).

Faithful Websites and Podcasts Addressing Contemporary Issues

Book of Mormon Central – "Build[ing] enduring faith in Jesus Christ by making the Book of Mormon accessible, comprehensible, and defensible to the entire world." http://www.bookofmormoncentral.org.

FairMormon – "FairMormon is a non-profit organization dedicated to providing well-documented answers to criticisms of LDS doctrine, belief and practice." http://www.fairmormon.org.

FaithMatters – "Matters Foundation aims to create a community in which an expansive view of the restored gospel can be considered and discussed." http://www.faithmatters.org.

Latter-day Saint Perspectives – "Latter-day Saint Perspectives is a twice-monthly podcast featuring interviews with respected scholars about Latter-day Saint history, doctrine, and culture." http://www.latterdaysaintperspectives.com.

LeadingSaints – "Be a Leader, Not a Calling." http://www.leadingsaints.org.

Listen Learn and Love – "Listen, Learn, and Love was created out of the desire to better understand our LGBTQ+ brothers and sisters." http://www.listen-learnandlove.org.

Neil A. Maxwell Institute Podcast – "Bringing discussions about faith and scholarship from BYU's Maxwell Institute straight to your ears." https://mi.byu.edu/mipodcast/.

For an updated list of resources visit http://www.bridgeslds.com/resources.

Notes

Introduction

1. See, for example, Patrick Q. Mason, *Planted: Belief and Belonging in an Age of Doubt* (Salt Lake City: Deseret Book, 2015); Terryl Givens and Fiona Givens, *The Crucible of Doubt: Reflections on the Quest of Faith* (Salt Lake City: Deseret Book, 2014); Adam S. Miller, *Letters to a Young Mormon*, 2nd ed. (Salt Lake City: Deseret Book, 2018); and Bruce C. Hafen and Marie K. Hafen, *Faith Is Not Blind* (Salt Lake City: Deseret Book, 2018).

2. The May 2018 "Local Leader Survey Regarding Faith Crisis," referred to as the *Local Leader Survey* throughout this book, was distributed to newsletter subscribers from LeadingSaints, a nonprofit that provides leadership tools to ward and stake leaders. The survey was administered on the SurveyMonkey platform and asked participants to respond to eight questions and sixty-seven statements about them, their faith, and their understanding of a faith crisis. I received 602 responses, of which 514 met the selection criteria of actively attending church and holding a current leadership calling. Eighty-eight percent of the respondents live in the United States. The leadership survey has broad age, gender, and geographic representation.

3. The September 2018 "Membership Survey Regarding Faith Crisis," referred to as the *Faith Crisis Member Survey* through this book, was distributed to members of a social media group of members who are in a faith crisis but working to remain positively engaged with the Church. The survey was administered on the SurveyMonkey platform and asked participants to respond to three questions and their agreement with seventy statements about them, their faith, and their understanding of a faith crisis. I received 423 responses, of which 320 met the selection criteria of being in a current faith crisis. I compared each age, gender, and geographic group for consistency with other information, including the Pew 2014 Survey on Religion, "Religions," *Pew Research Center*, https://www.pewforum.org/religious-landscape-study/; and the Jana Riess and Benjamin Knoll's article, "'Infected with Doubt': An Empirical Overview of Belief and Non-Belief in Contemporary Mormonism," *Dialogue: A Journal of Mormon Thought* 50, no. 3 (Fall 2017): 1–38. The results are consistent with data and expectations. While the data do not allow me to claim with utmost confidence that the results are fully representative of these groups, there is good reason to think that these results are not significantly off-base either. I believe these results are "ballpark" estimates but should be used with caution. While the results point to clear conclusions, they also point to areas for further research and analysis.

4. This group was formed in July 2018 and included eighty-three participants, recruited in the same social media group who later responded to the *Faith Crisis Member Survey*. They gave me permission to quote them anonymously.

5. Richard Lyman Bushman, "Finding the Right Words: Speaking Faith in Secular Times," in *Annual Report 2016–2017* (Provo, UT: Neal A. Maxwell Institute for Religious Education, 2017).

Chapter 1

1. Donald P. McNeill, Douglas A. Morrison, and Henri J. M. Nouwen, *Compassion: A Reflection on the Christian Life* (New York: Image Books, 1983), 4.

2. In question 9 of the *Local Leader Survey*, 97 percent of respondents indicated that they have a child, immediate family member, extended family, or close family member that have had or are in a faith crisis.

3. Darren E. Sherkat, *Changing Faith: The Dynamics and Consequences of Americans' Shifting Religious Identities* (New York: NYU Press, 2014).

4. Pew Research Center, *Religious Landscape Study*, accessed June 1, 2019, http://pewforum.org/religious-landscape-study/.

5. Benjamin Knoll and Jana Riess, "'Infected with Doubt': An Empirical Overview of Belief and Non-Belief in Contemporary American Mormonism," *Dialogue: A Journal of Mormon Thought* 50, no. 3 (Fall 2017): 1–37; Jana Riess, *The Next Mormons: How Millennials Are Changing the LDS Church* (New York: Oxford University Press, 2019).

6. Dareen E. Sherkat, *Changing Faith: The Dynamics and Consequences of Americans' Shifting Religious Identities* (New York City: New York University Press, 2014), tables 2.2, 2.3, and 2.6.

7. Sherkat, 62.

8. Riess, *Next Mormons*, 5.

9. Pew Research Center, *Religious Landscape Study*.

10. According to Pew, in 2007, 1.7 percent of the US adult population identified as Latter-day Saint (LDS); another 0.51 percent identified as former LDS. In 2014, 1.6 percent of the US adult population identified as LDS; 0.61 percent identified as former LDS. Applying Pew's findings to population numbers taken from US Census data, in 2007, of the 227.2 million adults in the United States, 3.86 million adults identified as LDS and 1.16 million as former LDS. In 2014, of the 247.2 million adults in the country, 3.92 million adults identified as LDS and 1.52 million as former LDS. This means that in 2014, approximately 360,000 more adults identified as former LDS than in 2007.

11. Knoll and Riess, "Infected with Doubt," 1–37.

12. The Cumorah Project, "Statistical Profile," accessed January 12, 2019, https://www.cumorah.com/index.php?target=countries&cnt_res=2&wid=231&wid_state=&cmdfind=Search.

13. Stephen R. Covey, *7 Habits of Highly Effective People* (New York: Simon and Schuster, 1989), 249.

14. The details and quotes in the personal stories told throughout this book were obtained during personal interviews that I held with each of these individuals. I have changed their names. The interviews took place between July 1, 2018, and September 30, 2018, and the transcripts of the interviews are in my possession.

15. Marlin K. Jensen, "Questions and Answers," devotional address, Utah State University, Logan, UT, November 2011.

16. Jeffrey R. Holland, "Songs Sung and Unsung," general conference address, April 2017, https://www.churchofjesuschrist.org/study/general-conference/2017/04/songs-sung-and-unsung.

17. M. Russell Ballard, "To Whom Shall I Go?", general conference address, October 2016, https://www.churchofjesuschrist.org/study/general-conference/2016/10/to-whom-shall-we-go.

18. Dieter F. Uchtdorf, "Come, Join with Us," general conference address, October 2013, https://www.churchofjesuschrist.org/study/general-conference/2013/10/come-join-with-us.

19. Dieter F. Uchtdorf, "Receiving a Testimony of Light and Truth," general conference address, October 2014, https://www.churchofjesuschrist.org/study/general-conference/2014/10/receiving-a-testimony-of-light-and-truth.

20. The Joseph Smith Papers Project, https://www.josephsmithpapers.org/.

21. Jean B. Bingham, "Ministering as the Savior Does," general conference address, April 2018, https://www.churchofjesuschrist.org/study/general-conference/2018/04/ministering-as-the-savior-does.

22. Jeffrey R. Holland, "Be with and Strengthen Them," general conference address, April 2018, https://www.churchofjesuschrist.org/study/general-conference/2018/04/be-with-and-strengthen-them.

Chapter 2

1. M. Russell Ballard, "The Opportunities and Responsibilities of CES Teachers in the 21st Century," address to CES religious educators, Salt Lake Tabernacle, Salt Lake City, February 26, 2016, https://www.churchofjesuschrist.org/broadcasts/article/evening-with-a-general-authority/2016/02/the-opportunities-and-responsibilities-of-ces-teachers-in-the-21st-century.

2. Bruce Drake, "6 New Findings about Millennials," Pew Research Center, March 7, 2014, https://www.pewresearch.org/fact-tank/2014/03/07/6-new-findings-about-millennials/.

3. Sarah Landrum, "Millennials Aren't Afraid to Change Jobs, And Here's Why," Forbes, November 10, 2017, https://www.forbes.com/sites/sarahlandrum/2017/11/10/millennials-arent-afraid-to-change-jobs-and-heres-why.

4. "2014 US Religious Landscape Study," Pew Research Center, May 12, 2015, https://www.pewforum.org/religious-landscape-study/generational-cohort/younger-millennial/.

5. Jana Riess, *The Next Mormons: How Millennials Are Changing the LDS Church* (New York: Oxford University Press, 2019), 9.

6. Drake, "6 New Findings about Millennials."

7. Drake.

8. "How Millennials Today Compare with Their Grandparents 50 Years Ago," Pew Research Center, March 17, 2015, https://www.pewresearch.org/fact-tank/2018/03/16/how-millennials-compare-with-their-grandparents/ft_millennials-education_031715/.

9. "How Millennials Today Compare."

10. Tim Henderson, "For Many Millennials, Marriage Can Wait," *Pew*, December 20, 2016, https://www.pewtrusts.org/en/research-and-analysis/blogs/stateline/2016/12/20/for-many-millennials-marriage-can-wait.

11. George Gao, "American's Ideal Family Size Is Smaller Than It Used to Be," *Pew Research Center*, May 8, 2015, https://www.pewresearch.org/fact-tank/2015/05/08/ideal-size-of-the-american-family/.

12. Jean M. Twenge, "The Real Reason Religion Is Declining in America," *Psychology Today*, May 27, 2015, https://www.psychologytoday.com/us/blog/our-changing-culture/201505/the-real-reason-religion-is-declining-in-america.

13. Joe Pinsker, "The Not-So-Great Reason Divorce Rates Are Declining," *The Atlantic*, September 25, 2018, https://www.theatlantic.com/family/archive/2018/09/millennials-divorce-baby-boomers/571282.

14. Jennifer Betts, "Historical Divorce Rate Statistics," *Love to Know*, accessed June 1, 2019, https://divorce.lovetoknow.com/Historical_Divorce_Rate_Statistics.

15. Danielle Sabrina, "Rising Trend: Social Responsibility Is High on Millennials' List," *Huffington Post*, February 3, 2017, https://www.huffingtonpost.com/danielle-sabrina/rising-trend-social-respo_b_14578380.html.

16. Josh Lews, "Men, Even More Than Women, Are Leaving Jobs for Work-Life Balance," LinkedIn, January 9, 2017, https://www.linkedin.com/pulse/men-even-more-than-women-leaving-jobs-work-life-balance-josh-levs/.

17. "Trends in Party Identification, 1939–2014," Pew Research Center, April 7, 2015, http://people-press.org/interactives/party-id-trend/.

18. "America's Changing Religious Landscape," Pew Research Center, May 12, 2015, http://pewforum.org/2015/05/12/americas-changing-religious-landscape/.

19. Ballard, "The Opportunities and Responsibilities of CES Teachers."

Chapter 3

1. Dieter F. Uchtdorf, "Come, Join with Us," general conference address, October 2013, https://www.churchofjesuschrist.org/study/general-conference/2013/10/come-join-with-us.

2. Researchers have studied why people leave a religion, and I have found useful the following studies: Dareen E. Sherkat, *Changing Faith: The Dynamics and Consequences of Americans' Shifting Religious Identities* (New York: NYU Press, 2014); Robert Wuthnow, *Inventing American Religion* (Oxford: Oxford University Press, 2015); Robert P. Jones, Daniel Cox, Betsy Cooper, and Rachel Lienesch, *Exodus, Why Americans Are Leaving Religion—and Why They're Unlikely to Come Back* (Washington,

DC: Public Religion Research Institute, 2016); Michael Lipka, "Why America's 'Nones' Left Religion Behind," Pew Research Center, August 24, 2016, http://pewresearch.org/fact-tank/2016/08/24/why-americas-nones-left-religion-behind/.

3. *Our Heritage: A Brief History of The Church of Jesus Christ of Latter-Day Saints* (Salt Lake City: The Church of Jesus Christ of Latter-day Saints, 1996).

4. *Doctrine and Covenants and Church History: Gospel Doctrine Teacher's Manual* (Salt Lake City: The Church of Jesus Christ of Latter-day Saints, 1999). See page 182 for the sole reference to Joseph Smith's practice of plural marriage: "In this dispensation, the Lord commanded some of the early Saints to practice plural marriage. The Prophet Joseph Smith and those closest to him, including Brigham Young and Heber C. Kimball, were challenged by this command, but they obeyed it."

5. *Saints: The Story of the Church of Jesus Christ in the Latter Days: The Standard of Trust: 1815-1845* (Salt Lake City: The Church of Jesus Christ of Latter-day Saints, 2018).

6. See Gregory A. Prince, *Gay Rights and the Mormon Church* (Salt Lake City: The University of Utah Press, 2019).

7. In a September 2015 *Ensign* article, Elder M. Russell Ballard wrote, "Let us be clear: The Church of Jesus Christ of Latter-day Saints believes that 'the experience of same-sex attraction is a complex reality for many people. The attraction itself is not a sin,' but acting on it is. Even though individuals do not choose to have such attractions, they do choose how to respond to them." M. Russell Ballard, "The Lord Needs You Now!," *Ensign*, September 2015, https://www.churchofjesuschrist.org/study/ensign/2015/09/the-lord-needs-you-now.html.

8. Lee Hale, "Can the LDS Church Be Blamed for Utah's LGBT Suicides?", KUER, July 25, 2018, https://www.kuer.org/post/can-lds-church-be-blamed-utah-s-lgbt-suicides.

9. Caitlin Ryan, as quoted in Prince, *Gay Rights and the Mormon Church*, 210.

10. Jacob J. Gates, "In U.S., More Adults Identifying as LGBT," Gallup, January 11, 2017, https://news.gallup.com/poll/201731/lgbt-identification-rises.aspx.

11. M. Russell Ballard, "Questions and Answers," devotional address, Brigham Young University, Provo, UT, November 14, 2017, https://speeches.byu.edu/talks/m-russell-ballard_questions-and-answers/.

12. Neylan McBaine, *Women at Church: Magnifying LDS Women's Local Impact* (Salt Lake City: Greg Kofford Books, 2014), xiiv.

13. McBaine, 42

14. See Thomas Burr, "Mormon Bishops Told Ex-Wives of Former Hatch, White House Staffer to Consider His 'Career Ambitions' When They Reported His Physical Abuse, They Say," *Salt Lake Tribune*, February 9, 2018, https://www.sltrib.com/news/politics/2018/02/08/white-house-officials-ex-wives-say-their-mormon-bishops-were-no-help-when-they-were-abused/.

15. "Stake President Denies Temple Recommend to Nursing Mother," *Exponent II* (blog), August 5, 2018, https://www.the-exponent.com/stake-president-denies -temple-recommend-to-nursing-mother/.

16. See Dallin H. Oaks, "The Keys and Authority of the Priesthood," general conference address, April 2014, https://https://www.churchofjesuschrist.org/ study/general-conference/2014/04/the-keys-and-authority-of-the-priesthood.

17. Carol Lynn Pearson, *The Ghost of Eternal Polygamy* (Walnut Creek, CA: Pivot Point Books, 2016), 24–25.

18. Jana Riess, "How to Create Ex-Mormons," Religion News Service, February 25, 2018, https://religionnews.com/2018/02/05/how-to-create-ex-mormons/.

19. Benjamin Knoll and Jana Riess, "'Infected with Doubt': An Empirical Overview of Belief and Non-Belief in Contemporary American Mormonism," *Dialogue: A Journal of Mormon Thought* 50, no. 3 (Fall 2017).

20. The Church of Jesus Christ of Latter-day Saints, "Political Neutrality," Newsroom, https://newsroom.churchofjesuschrist.org/ldsnewsroom/eng/public-issues/political -neutrality

21. Sherkat found that Latter-day Saints who identified as Republican rose from about 52 percent for those born prior to 1944, to 62.3 percent for those born between 1945 and 1955, to 70.9 percent for those born between 1956 and 1970, and to 76.6 percent for those born after 1970. No other American religion has had this kind of generational shift toward conservatism. Sherkat, *Changing Faith*, 170.

22. Jana Riess, *The Next Mormons: How Millennials Are Changing the LDS Church* (New York: Oxford University Press, 2019).

23. "Mental Illness," *National Institute of Mental Health*, updated November 2017, https://www.nimh.nih.gov/health/statistics/mental-illness.shtml.

24. Jane Clayson Johnson, *Silent Souls Weeping* (Salt Lake City: Deseret Book, 2018), 6.

25. Jeffrey R. Holland, "Like a Broken Vessel," general conference address, October 2013, https://www.churchofjesuschrist.org/study/general-conference/ 2013/10/like-a-broken-vessel.

26. Riess, *Next Mormons*, 17.

27. Riess, 20.

28. This is higher than the 43.6 percent of believers who said in an earlier survey that they read their scriptures daily. Knoll and Riess, "Infected with Doubt."

29. Thomas G. Plante, "Giving People Advice Rarely Works. This Does," *Psychology Today*, July 15, 2014, https://www.psychologytoday.com/us/blog/ do-the-right-thing/201407/giving-people-advice-rarely-works-does.

30. Plante.

Chapter 4

1. Jeffrey R. Holland, "Bearing One Another's Burdens," Prophets and Apostles, The Church of Jesus Christ of Latter-day Saints, accessed June 27, 2019,

https://www.churchofjesuschrist.org/prophets-and-apostles/unto-all-the-world/bearing-one-anothers-burdens.

2. The Gospel Topics Essays can be found at https://www.churchofjesuschrist.org/manual/gospel-topics-essays. The Joseph Smith Papers can be accessed at https://www.josephsmithpapers.org; and the *Saints* volume can be found at https://history.churchofjesuschrist.org/saints The Gospel Topics Essays and *Saints* are also found in the Church history section of the Gospel Library app.

3. M. Russell Ballard, "The Opportunities and Responsibilities of CES Teachers in the 21st Century," address to CES religious educators, Salt Lake Tabernacle, Salt Lake City, February 26, 2016, https://www.churchofjesuschrist.org/broadcasts/article/evening-with-a-general-authority/2016/02/the-opportunities-and-responsibilities-of-ces-teachers-in-the-21st-century.

4. For those who want to learn more or reference primary sources, the essays cite those as well as scholarly works for more in-depth study.

5. Patrick Mason, personal conversation with author, September 11, 2018.

6. Ballard, "The Opportunities and Responsibilities of CES Teachers."

7. Blair Hodges, "Truth in Church History: Excerpts from the *Religious Educator's* Q&A with Elder Steven Snow," BYU Maxwell Institute, November 8, 2013, https://mi.byu.edu/truth-in-church-history-excerpts-from-the-religious-educators-qa-with-elder-steven-snow/.

8. Patrick Mason, personal conversation with author, September 11, 2018.

9. *Handbook 2: Administering the Church* (Salt Lake City: The Church of Jesus Christ of Latter-day Saints, 2010), section 1.2.2.

10. *Preach My Gospel: A Guide to Missionary Service* (Salt Lake City: The Church of Jesus Christ of Latter-day Saints, 2004), 1.

11. *Handbook 2: Administering the Church*, section 1.1.4.

12. *Preach My Gospel: A Guide to Missionary Service* (Salt Lake City: The Church of Jesus Christ of Latter-day Saints, 2018), 115–26.

13. *Preach My Gospel* (2018), 117.

14. *Preach My Gospel* (2018), 118.

15. *Preach My Gospel* (2018), 120.

16. The Church of Jesus Christ of Latter-day Saints, "Race and the Church: All Are Alike unto God," Newsroom, February 29, 2012, https://newsroom.churchofjesuschrist.org/article/race-church.

17. B. H. Roberts, "Elation of Inspiration and Revelation to Church Government," *Improvement Era,* March 1905, 365–66.

18. Terryl Givens and Fiona Givens, *The Crucible of Doubt* (Salt Lake City: Deseret Book, 2014), 70.

19. Patrick Mason, "The Courage of Our Convictions: Embracing Mormonism in a Secular Age," lecture, FairMormon Conference, 2016, https://www.fairmormon.org/conference/august-2016/courage-convictions.

20. *Preach My Gospel* (2018), 1.

21. Compare the title page in the 1981 edition of the Book of Mormon to the title page in the 2018 edition.

22. See "Book of Mormon and DNA Studies," Gospel Topics Essays, The Church of Jesus Christ of Latter-day Saints, 2016, https://www.churchofjesuschrist.org/study/manual/gospel-topics-essays/book-of-mormon-and-dna-studies.

23. "Mormons Free to Back Gay Marriage on Social Media, LDS Apostle Reiterates," *Salt Lake Tribune*, March 17, 2015, https://archive.sltrib.com/article.php?id=2301174&itype=CMSID.

24. Jeffrey R. Holland, "Lord, I Believe," general conference address, April 2013, https://www.churchofjesuschrist.org/study/general-conference/2013/04/lord-i-believe.

25. Neil L. Andersen, "You Know Enough," general conference address, October 2008, https://www.churchofjesuschrist.org/study/general-conference/2008/10/you-know-enough.

26. Bruce C. Hafen and Marie K. Hafen, *Faith Is Not Blind* (Salt Lake City: Deseret Book, 2018), 13.

27. Quoted in *Teachings of the Presidents of the Church: Howard W. Hunter* (Salt Lake City: The Church of Jesus Christ of Latter-day Saints, 2015), 270.

28. LDS Living, "Belief & Doubt: 'We Need to Make Room for, 'I Believe, I Hope, I Trust.'" -Terryl's Story," Youtube, January 23, 2018, https://youtu.be/0SY85KR5xi8.

29. Dieter F. Uchtdorf, "Come, Join with Us," general conference address, October 2013, https://www.churchofjesuschrist.org/study/general-conference/2013/10/come-join-with-us.

30. *True to the Faith* (Salt Lake City: The Church of Jesus Christ of Latter-day Saints, 2004), 54.

Chapter 5

1. Patricia P. Pinegar, "Increase in Faith," general Young Women meeting address, April 1994, https://www.churchofjesuschrist.org/study/general-conference/1994/04/increase-in-faith.

2. Jeffery R. Holland, "Lord, I Believe," general conference address, April 2013, https://www.churchofjesuschrist.org/study/general-conference/2013/04/lord-i-believe.

3. Terryl and Fiona Givens, *The God Who Weeps: How Mormonism Makes Sense of Life* (Crawfordsville, IN: Ensign Peak, 2012), 25.

4. Samuel B. Hislop, "We Aren't God's Only People," The Church of Jesus Christ of Latter-day Saints, October 27, 2016, https://www.churchofjesuschrist.org/blog/we-arent-gods-only-people.

5. Philip L. Barlow, "Questing and Questioning," *Sunstone*, November 26, 2014, https://sunstonemagazine.com/questing-and-questioning.

6. James W. Fowler, *Stages of Faith: The Psychology of Human Development and the Quest for Meaning* (New York: Harper Collins, 1981), 151.

7. Fowler, 174.

8. Thomas Wirthlin McConkie, *Navigating Mormon Faith Crisis* (West Valley City, UT: Sun Print Solutions, 2015), 2.

9. "Dark Night of the Soul," Wikipedia, updated November 9, 2018, https://en.wikipedia.org/wiki/Dark_Night_of_the_Soul.

10. McConkie, *Navigating Mormon Faith Crisis*, 2.

11. James Martin, "A Saint's Dark Night," *New York Times*, August 29, 2007, https://www.nytimes.com/2007/08/29/opinion/29martin.html.

12. Brigham Young, March 29, 1868, *Journal of Discourses*, 26 vols. (London and Liverpool: LDS Booksellers Depot, 1854–86), 12:168.

Chapter 6

1. Barbara B. Smith, "A Safe Place for Marriages and Families," general conference address, October 1981, https://www.churchofjesuschrist.org/study/general-conference/1981/10/a-safe-place-for-marriages-and-families.

2. Marlin K. Jensen, "Questions and Answers," devotional address, Utah State University, Logan, UT, November 2011.

3. Henry B. Eyring, "Bind Up Their Wounds," general conference address, November 2013, https://www.churchofjesuschrist.org/study/general-conference/2013/10/bind-up-their-wounds.

4. John Taylor, "The Organization of the Church," *Millennial Star*, November 15, 1851, 339.

5. Terryl Givens and Fiona Givens, *The Crucible of Doubt* (Salt Lake City: Deseret Book, 2014), 70.

Chapter 7

1. Jean B. Bingham, "Focus on the One," video, *Unity in Diversity*, LDS Media Library, https://www.churchofjesuschrist.org/media-library/video/2016-03-0024-focus-on-the-one.

2. "The Church of Jesus Christ," *Children's Songbook* (Salt Lake City: The Church of Jesus Christ of Latter-day Saints, 1989), 77.

3. Brené Brown, *Braving the Wilderness. The Quest for True Belonging and the Courage to Stand Alone* (New York: Random House, 2017), 160.

4. Marlin K. Jensen, "A Disciple's Plea for Openness and Inclusion," interview by Terryl Givens, Faith Matters, November 21, 2017, https://faithmatters.org/a-disciples-plea-for-openness-and-inclusion-an-interview-with-elder-marlin-k-jensen/.

5. LDS Living, "Belief & Doubt: 'We Need to Make Room for, 'I Believe, I Hope, I Trust." -Terryl's Story," Youtube, January 23, 2018, https://youtu.be/0SY85KR5xi8.

6. Tom Christofferson, *That We May Be One: A Gay Mormon's Perspective on Faith and Family* (Salt Lake City: Deseret Book, 2017), 19.

7. Christofferson, 19.

8. Christofferson, 19.

9. M. Russell Ballard, "To Whom Shall We Go," general conference address, October 2013, https://www.churchofjesuschrist.org/study/general-conference/2016/10/to-whom-shall-we-go.

10. M. Russell Ballard, "To the Saints in the Utah South Area," Prophets and Apostles, The Church of Jesus Christ of Latter-day Saints, accessed June 27, 2019, https://www.churchofjesuschrist.org/prophets-and-apostles/unto-all-the-world/to-the-saints-in-the-utah-south-area.

11. Joan Halifax, *Being with Dying: Cultivating Compassion and Fearlessness in the Presence of Death* (Boston: Shambhala Publications, 2008), 17.

12. Orson F. Whitney, April 7, 1929, *Ninety-Ninth Annual Conference of The Church of Jesus Christ of Latter-day Saints* (Salt Lake City: The Church of Jesus Christ of Latter-day Saints, 1929), 109.

13. Bingham, "Focus on the One."

Chapter 8

1. Rabbi David J. Wolpe, "Why Faith Matters" lecture, Emory University, Atlanta, GA, October 21, 2008, quoted in The Church of Jesus Christ of Latter-day Saints, "Why Religion Matters: The Longing Within," Newsroom, February, 10, 2014, https://newsroom.churchofjesuschrist.org/article/why-religion-matters-longing-within.

2. Pat Fleming, "Each Moment Is Precious," Family Friend Poems, October 29, 2018, https://www.familyfriendpoems.com/poem/each-moment-is-precious.

3. Terryl Givens and Fiona Givens, *The God Who Weeps: How Mormonism Makes Sense of Life* (Crawfordsville, IN: Ensign Peak, 2012), 6–7.

4. "I Am a Child of God," *Hymns* (Salt Lake City: The Church of Jesus Christ of Latter-day Saints, 1985), hymn 301.

5. Jana Riess, *The Next Mormons: How Millennials Are Changing the LDS Church* (New York: Oxford University Press, 2019).

6. "Where Can I Turn for Peace?" *Hymns* (Salt Lake City: The Church of Jesus Christ of Latter-day Saints, 1985), hymn 129.

7. Abraham Joshua Heschel, *God in Search of Man: A Philosophy of Judaism* (New York: Farrar, Straus and Girous, 1955).

Chapter 9

1. Ann E. Tanner, "Carrying Others to the Pool of Bethesda," *Ensign*, January 2011, https://www.churchofjesuschrist.org/study/ensign/2011/01/carrying-others-to-the-pool-of-bethesda.

2. "What Is Ministering," The Church of Jesus Christ of Latter-day Saints, updated September 1, 2018, https://www.churchofjesuschrist.org/ministering/what-is-ministering.

3. Brené Brown, *Daring Greatly: How the Courage to Be Vulnerable Transforms the Way We Live, Love, Parent and Lead* (New York: Penguin Random House, 2012), 148.

4. Eric D. Huntsman, "Hard Sayings and Safe Spaces: Making Room for Struggle as Well as Faith," devotional address, Brigham Young University, Provo, UT, August 7, 2018, https://speeches.byu.edu/talks/eric-d-huntsman_hard-sayings-and-safe-spaces-making-room-for-both-struggle-and-faith/.

5. Sheldon Lawrence, "The Coddling of the Mormon Mind: On Spiritual Trigger Warnings and Religious Safe Spaces," Dawning of a Brighter Day (blog), Association of Mormon Letters, October 3, 2016, https://associationmormonletters.org/blog/2016/10/the-coddling-of-the-mormon-mind-on-spiritual-trigger-warnings-and-religious-safe-spaces/.

6. Brendan Vaughn, "Rogers and Me," New York Times, September 10, 2006, https://www.nytimes.com/2006/09/10/books/review/Vaughan.t.html.

7. Ralph G. Nichols, Are you Listening (New York: McGraw Hill Book Company, 1957).

8. Ralph G. Nichols, "The Struggle to Be Human," keynote address, first annual convention of the International Listening Association, February 17, 1980.

9. Popular quotation attributed to L. J. Isham.

10. "Oprah Talks to Tich Nhat Hanh," Oprah.com, March 2010, http://www.oprah.com/spirit/oprah-talks-to-thich-nhat-hanh/.

11. Janet Dunn, "How to Become a Good Listener," Desiring God, April 1, 1983, https://www.desiringgod.org/articles/how-to-become-a-good-listener.

12. The Arbinger Institute, The Anatomy of Peace (Oakland, CA: Berrett-Koehler, 2006), 34.

13. Stephen R. Covey, The Seven Habits of Highly Effective People (New York: Simon and Schuster, 2004), 239.

14. Adam S. Miller, "Op-ed: Listening Is the First Step in Speaking to Mormon Millennials," Deseret News, December 17, 2017, https://www.deseretnews.com/article/865694056/Op-ed-Listening-is-the-first-step-in-speaking-to-Mormon-millennials.html.

15. M. Russell Ballard, "Questions and Answers," devotional address, Brigham Young University, Provo, UT, November 14, 2017, https://speeches.byu.edu/talks/m-russell-ballard_questions-and-answers/.

16. See, for example, Thomas G. Plante, "Giving People Advice Rarely Works. This Does," Psychology Today, July 15, 2014, https://www.psychologytoday.com/us/blog/do-the-right-thing/201407/giving-people-advice-rarely-works-does.

17. Parker J. Palmer, "The Gift of Presence, The Perils of Advice," On Being (blog), April 27, 2016, https://onbeing.org/blog/the-gift-of-presence-the-perils-of-advice/.

18. Celeste Headlee, "The Mistake I Made with My Grieving Friends," Oprah.com, https://www.oprah.com/inspiration/celeste-headlee-the-mistake-i-made-with-my-grieving-friend.

19. Sandra Rogers, "Hearts Knit Together," in Hearts Knit Together: Talks from the 1995 Women's Conference (Provo, UT: Brigham Young University, 1996), 7.

20. Rogers, 7–8.

21. Jana Riess, "Undoing the Culture of Mormon Judgmentalism—Or, I Am Not a 'Tare,'" *Religion News Service*, November 13, 2018, https://religionnews.com/2018/11/13/undoing-the-culture-of-mormon-judgmentalism-or-i-am-not-a-tare/.

22. Elder Dale G. Renlund, "Through God's Eyes," general conference address, October 2015, https://www.churchofjesuschrist.org/study/general-conference/2015/10/through-gods-eyes.

23. Jeffrey R. Holland, "Bearing One Another's Burdens," Prophets and Apostles, The Church of Jesus Chirst of Latter-day Saints, updated September 1, 2018, https://www.churchofjesuschrist.org/prophets-and-apostles/unto-all-the-world/bearing-one-anothers-burdens.

24. Roman Krznaric, "Six Habits of Highly Empathic People," *Greater Good Magazine*, November 27, 2012, https://greatergood.berkeley.edu/article/item/six_habits_of_highly_empathic_people1.

25. Brené Brown, *Daring Greatly,* 81.

26. Kyle Benson, "The Magic Ratio, According to Science," The Gottman Institute, October 4, 2017, https://www.gottman.com/blog/the-magic-relationship-ratio-according-science/.

27. John M. Gottman, "The Roles of Conflict Engagement, Escalation or Avoidance in Marital Interactions: A Longitudinal View of Five Types of Couples," *Journal of Consulting & Clinical Psychology* 61, no. 1 (1993): 6–15.

28. John M. Gottman, *The Science of Trust: Emotional Attunement for Couples* (New York: W. W. Norton, 2011), 63, 17–21.

29. Gottman, *Science of Trust*, 17–21.

30. Karyn Hall, "Understanding Validation: A Way to Communicate Acceptance," *Psychology Today*, April 26, 2012, https://www.psychologytoday.com/au/blog/pieces-mind/201204/understanding-validation-way-communicate-acceptance.

Chapter 10

1. Carole M. Stephens, "The Family Is of God," general conference address, April 2015, https://www.churchofjesuschrist.org/study/general-conference/2015/04/the-family-is-of-god.

2. Dieter F. Uchtdorf, "Receiving a Testimony of Light and Truth," general conference address, October 2014, https://www.churchofjesuschrist.org/study/general-conference/2014/10/receiving-a-testimony-of-light-and-truth.

3. Joseph F. Smith, *Testimony before the Senate. The Seating of Senator Reed Smoot* (Washington, DC: Congressional Series of United States Public Documents, March 1904), vol. 4932, p. 98.

4. Dieter F. Uchtdorf, "Come, Join with Us," general conference address, October 2013, https://www.churchofjesuschrist.org/study/general-conference/2013/10/come-join-with-us.

5. Jeffrey R. Holland, "Songs Sung and Unsung," general conference address, April 2017, https://www.churchofjesuschrist.org/study/general-conference/2017/04/songs-sung-and-unsung.

6. Brené Brown, *Daring Greatly: How the Courage to Be Vulnerable Transforms the Way We Live, Love, Parent and Lead* (New York: Penguin Random House, 2012), 187

7. M. Russell Ballard, "To the Saints in the Utah South Area," Prophets and Apostles, The Church of Jesus Christ of Latter-day Saints, accessed June 27, 2019, https://www.churchofjesuschrist.org/prophets-and-apostles/unto-all-the-world/to-the-saints-in-the-utah-south-area.

8. Joseph Smith et al., *History of the Church of Jesus Christ of Latter-day Saints*, ed. B. H. Roberts, 7 vols., 2nd ed. rev. (Salt Lake City: Deseret Book, 1957), 5:340.

9. Merriam-Webster, s.v. "worthiness," accessed January 5, 2019, https://www.merriam-webster.com/dictionary/worthiness.

10. Brené Brown, "Shame v. Guilt," Brené Brown (blog), January 14, 2013, https://brenebrown.com/blog/2013/01/14/shame-v-guilt/.

11. Brené Brown, "Listening to Shame," Ted Talk, March 2012, https://www.ted.com/talks/brene_brown_listening_to_shame/transcript.

12. Dieter F. Uchtdorf, "The Love of God," general conference address, October 2009, https://www.churchofjesuschrist.org/study/general-conference/2009/10/the-love-of-god.

13. Richard Ostler, "We Need to Stop Judging Each Other and Our Righteousness Based on Church Callings," *LDS Living*, accessed January 4, 2019, http://www.ldsliving.com/We-Need-to-Stop-Judging-Each-Other-and-Our-Righteousness-Based-on-Church-Callings/s/85828.

14. Letter, July 31, 2015, in possession of Richard Ostler.

15. Jana Riess, *The Next Mormons: How Millennials Are Changing the LDS Church* (New York: Oxford University Press, 2019), 99.

16. Rachel Hunt Steenblik, *Mother's Milk: Poems in Search of Heavenly* Mother (Salt Lake City: By Common Consent Press, 2017), 15.

17. Henry Wadsworth Longfellow, "The Courtship of Miles Standish." Henry Wadsworth Longfellow, Maine Historical Society, accessed June 11, 2019, https://www.hwlongfellow.org/poems_poem.php?pid=191.

18. *Saints: The Story of the Church of Jesus Christ in the Latter Days* (Salt Lake City: The Church of Jesus Christ of Latter-day Saints, 2018); *At the Pulpit: 185 Years of Discourses by Latter-day Saint Women* (Salt Lake City: Church Historian's Press, 2017).

19. Steenblik, *Mother's Milk*, 14.

20. Neylan McBaine, *Women at Church, Magnifying LDS Women's Local Impact* (Greg Kofford Books: Salt Lake City, 2014).

21. Dallin H. Oaks, "The Keys and Authority of the Priesthood," general conference address, April 2014, https://www.churchofjesuschrist.org/study/general-conference/2014/04/the-keys-and-authority-of-the-priesthood.

22. Stephen L. Richards, in *One Hundred Twenty-Fourth Semiannual Conference of The Church of Jesus Christ of Latter-day Saints* (Salt Lake City: The Church of Jesus Christ of Latter-day Saints, October 1953), 86.

23. M. Russell Ballard, *Counseling with Our Councils* (Salt Lake City: Deseret Book, 2012).

24. M. Russel Ballard, "Strength in Councils," general conference address, October 1993, https://www.churchofjesuschrist.org/study/general-conference/1993/10/strength-in-counsel.

25. *Handbook 2: Administering the Church* (Salt Lake City: The Church of Jesus Christ of Latter-day Saints, 2018), section 18.2.2, https://www.churchofjesuschrist.org/study/manual/handbook-2-administering-the-church/title-page26. Bruce C. Hafen and Marie C. Hafen, *Faith Is Not Blind* (Salt Lake City: Deseret Book, 2018), 20.

27. Terryl Givens and Fiona Givens, *The Crucible of Doubt: Reflections on the Quest for Faith* (Salt Lake City: Deseret Book, 2014), 31.

Conclusion

1. Joy F. Evans, "Lord, When Saw We Thee an Hungered?," general conference address, April 1989, https://www.churchofjesuschrist.org/study/ensign/1989/05/lord-when-saw-we-thee-an-hungred.

2. Ashley Mae Hoiland, *One Hundred Birds Taught Me to Fly* (Provo, UT: A Living Faith Book, 2016), 70.

Index

#

1984, 133

A

Allison, 77–78
Alma the Younger, 67
Amanda, 9–10, 67–69, 158–59
Anatomy of Peace, 110–11
Anderson, Neal A., 58
anti-Mormon, 116
apostasy
  greatest since Kirtland, 15
  increasing, 4–5
apostate, 116
Ashley, 147–49
Atonement, xiv, 51–52, 56, 61–64, 89,
  91, 103
autism, 153

B

Ballard, M. Russell
  on belonging, 90–91
  discusses role of women, 34
  on Gospel Topics Essays, 48–49
  on inclusive councils, 151
  on LGBTQ inclusivity, 33
  on need to study, 23–24
  on open discussions, 135
  on transparency, 49
  on unwanted advice, 112–13
Barlow, Philip, 65–66
Bednar, David A., 118
belonging, 28
  at church, 86–88
  creating space for, 90
  at home, 88–90
  understanding, 85–86

Bingham, Jean B.
  on ministering, 15
  on openness, 85, 92
Book of Mormon, 6–7, 144
bridges. *See also* ministering.
  purpose of, xii
  requirements, xii.
  two way, xii
Brown, Brené
  on belonging, 85
  on empathy, 122
  on loneliness, 103–4
  on policing, 133–34
  on shaming, 139
Bushman, Richard, xiii

C

Carly, 17
Christofferson, D. Todd, 57, 90
Christofferson, Tom, 90
Church history, 11, 28–30, 153
  need to study, 47–50
  transparency, 49–50
Church leaders (general)
  and Church bureaucracy, 39–40
  disagreeing with, 57
  limitations of, 11, 53–54, 61–63
  losing trust in, 75–79
  sustaining, 53–54
Church leaders (local)
  ability to address faith crises, 13–15
  assumptions about, 141–44
  know someone in faith crisis, 12
  lack of training, xi
  limitations of, 11, 61–63
  need to listen to women, 144–50
  responsibilities of, 82

church meetings
  for addressing concerns, 136–39
  councils, 150–51
  Gospel Topics Essays, 137
  include more perspectives, 150–51
  making inclusive, 130–36
  ministering in, 129–30
  policing, 133–36
  sacrament meeting, 151–54
Come Follow Me, 15
confidentiality, 77, 79
councils
  include LGTQ members, 151
  include more women, 150
  include needed perspectives, 150–51
Covey, Stephen R., 6, 111–12
cultural issues, 40–41

D–E

dark night of the soul, 67–69
disabilities, 153
divorce, 21
doctrines, 94, 96
Dunn, Janet, 107
Echo Hawk, Larry, 41
emotional challenges, 41–42
empathy, xii, 121–23
employment, 21–22
Enoch, 64
Evans, Joy F., 157
Eyring, Henry B., 80

F

faith
  living, 60
  stages of, 66–69
faith crises
  among close friends and family, 12
  avoiding, 47
  blaming, 8–9, 11, 43, 79, 118–19
  causes of, 9
  and Church history, 28
  dark night of the soul, 67–69

defined, x, 67–68
difficult to disclose, 8
and family, xii
hidden, x, 8, 11, 127–29
importance of addressing, 13
and the internet, 19–20, 22–25
isolating, 11, 103
need to understand, xi–xii
often irreversible, xii, 71, 160
reasons for, 118–19
and relationships, 10
sincerity of, 9
source of pain, xi–xii, 7–8, 70, 89
Faith Crisis Member Focus Group
  Church leaders, 77
  creating meaning, 98
  described, xi
  helpful leaders, 82–83
  judgement, 37
  labeling, 116–17
  policing, 133
  worthiness, 142–43
Faith Crisis Member Survey
  belonging, 86–87
  Church history, 28
  Church leaders, 75–76
  described, xi
  discussing issues, 129
  finding meaning at church, 95–96
  gender roles, 33–34
  Gospel Topics Essays, 30
  hidden faith crises, 127–28
  judgement, 37
  leaders' ability to address faith crises,
    14, 81
  LGBTQ issues, 31–32
  reasons for faith crises, 44
  religious practices, 43–44
  singles, 117
  trust, 29
family, 88
  changing views on, 95
feminism, 116–17

Flindt, Lisa, 117–18
Fowler, James W., 66–67
free agency, xii

G

gaslighting, 119–20
gender inequality, 33–36, 38
  polygamy, 35–36
  temple, 35
generational differences, 4–5
Givens, Fiona
  on divine sadness, 64
  on limitations of Church leaders,
    54, 80
  on unique doctrines, 93–94
Givens, Terryl L.
  on divine sadness, 64
  on doubt, 88
  on limitations of Church leaders,
    54, 80
  on uncertainty, 59
  on unique doctrines, 93–94
Gospel Topics Essays, 15, 48, 153
  in church meetings, 137
  underutilized, 30, 49–50
Gottman, John, 123

H

Hafen, Bruce C., 58
Hafen, Marie, 58
Halifax, Joan, 91
Hall, Karyn, 124
Heschel, Abraham, 97
Hislop, Samuel B., 65
Hoiland, Ashley Mae, 160
Holland, Jeffrey R.
  on being more inclusive, 131
  on depression, 42
  on empathy, 121
  on limitations of Church leaders, 62
  on nurturing faith, 57–58
  on pure religion, 15–16
  on self-care, 47

hope, 51
Hunter, Howard W., 58–59
Huntsman, Eric D., 104

I–K

internet, 19–20, 22–25
Jacob, 17
James, 81
Jensen, Marlin K.
  on apostasy, 14–15
  on not fitting the norm, 87–88
  on policing, 80
  on uncertainty, 80
Jesus Christ
  characteristics of, 51–52
  example of empathy, 122
  example of ministering, 103
  faith crisis, 67
  faith in, 51, 61
  focus on, 50–53, 98
Jim, 130
Joe, 142–43
Johnson, Jane Clayson, 42
Joseph Smith Papers, 15, 48
judging, 36–39, 44–45, 117–18
  blaming, 11, 43–45
Knoll, Benjamin, 3, 5, 36–37
Kristine, 32
Krznaric, Roman, 121–22

L

labeling, 8, 79, 115–17
  examples of, 116–17
language issues, 40–41
LeadingSaints, 12
Lehi's dream, 68–69
Levenson, Robert, 123
LGBTQ issues, 30–47, 90, 153
  councils, 151
  defined, 30
  harmful comments in church, 30
  November policy, 31
  Prop. 8, 31

listening, 79, 105–11
  alienating behaviors, 111–21
  importance of, 8, 157–59
  judging, 117–19
  making about ourselves, 114–15
  questions to ask, 105
  things to say, 109
  tips, 107–8
  unwanted advice, 112–14
  validating feelings, 110
  to women, 144–50
Local Leader Survey
  ability to address faith crises, 13–14, 81
  close friends and family, 12
  described, xi, 12
  Gospel Topics Essays, 30
  importance of addressing faith crises, 13
  personal belief, 128
  reasons for faith crises, 44
  wards addressing faith crises, 129
Longfellow, Henry Wordsworth, 145
love, 52
  God's, 64–66

religiosity of, 18, 22
religious loyalty, 4–5
and social justice, 18, 95
and trust, 19
unique issues, 43
women, 19
Miller, Adam, 112
ministering, 15
  at church, 127–55
  church meetings for, 129–30
  councils, 150–51
  defined, 103
  effective, xii
  empathy, xii, 121–23
  key principles, 103–25
  listening. See listening.
  positivity, 123–24
  sacrament meeting, 151–54
  to those in faith crisis, 69–71
  through love, 104
  validating, 124–25
  vulnerability, xii
Mother Theresa, 68

M

manipulating, 119–20
Marriage, 21. See also divorce.
Mason, Patrick
  on studying Church history, 48, 50
  on truth carts, 55
McBaine, Neylan, 34, 146
McConkie, Thomas Wirthlin, 67–68
meaning, 28
  finding at church, 97–99
  losing at church, 95–97
  provided by gospel, 93–95
mental challenges, 41–42
Mike, 6–9, 24, 67–69, 157–58
millennials
  concerns of, 18
  defined, 17
  diverse, 18
  lower divorce rate, 21

N–O

Nhất Hạnh, Thích, 106–7
Nichols, Ralph G., 106
November 2015 policy, 31
Oaks, Dallin H., 147
objectifying, 110–11
Ordain Women, 33–34
Ostler, Richard, 142
Our Heritage, 28–29

P

patience, 52
personal stories, 6–10, 17, 24, 32,
  67–69, 77–78, 81, 130, 142–43,
  147–49, 157–59. *See also* Allison,
  Amanda, Ashley, Carly, Jacob, James,
  Jim, Joe, Kristine, Mike, Roger.
Pew Research Center, 3, 5, 17
policing, 38–39, 80, 133–36

politics, 22, 41
polygamy, 7, 24, 29, 35–36
Preach My Gospel, 51
priesthood and temple ban, 29, 53
Proposition 8, 31

R

racism, 53
Renlund, Dale G., 121
Richards, Stephen L., 151
Riess, Jana
    on burnout, 36–37
    on inclusivity, 19
    on millennials, 3–5
    on moral priorities, 95
    on political ideology, 41
    on women, 144
Roger, 89–90
Rogers, Fred, 105–6
Rogers, Sandra, 117–18

S

sacrament meeting, 151–54
Saints, 15, 29, 48
scripture study, 6–8
secret sin, 8, 119
seer stones, 29, 48
sexual abuse, 153
shelf, 9
Sherkat, Darren E., 3
Smith, Barbara, B., 75
Smith, Joseph
    faith crisis, 67
    on policing, 135–36
Smith, Joseph F., 130–31
Snow, Steve E., 50
social justice
    and millennials, 18, 95
    part of gospel, 97
spiritual growth, 54–56, 61–69, 71
stake leaders. *See* Church leaders (local).
Steenblick, Rachel Hunt, 145–46
Stephens, Carole M., 127

suffering, 63
switching, 4, 21–22

T

tares, 8, 119
technology, 19–20
temple, 35
testimony
    loss of, 6
    maturing 54–56, 61–69
thoughtcrime, 133
titles, 35
True to the Faith, 60
trust, 28
    among millennials, 19
    building, 79–83
    tailoring to individual, 83–84
truth cart, 54–57

U–V

Uchtdorf, Dieter F.
    on being more inclusive, 130–31
    on faith crises, 27
    on having questions, 60
uncertainty, 59–60
validating, 124–25

W

ward leaders. *See* Church leaders (local).
Waters of Mormon, xii, 6
Whitney, Orson F., 91
Wolpe, David, 93
women, 79
    in Book of Mormon, 144
    feminism, 116–17
    gender inequality, 33–36
    listening to, 144–50
    and priesthood, 33–34, 147–47
worthiness, 139–44

Also available from
GREG KOFFORD BOOKS

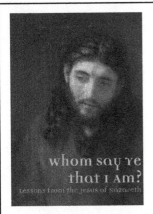

Whom Say Ye That I Am?
Lessons from
the Jesus of Nazareth

James W. McConkie
and Judith E. McConkie

Paperback, ISBN: 978-1-58958-707-6

"This book is the most important Jesus study to date written by believing Mormons for an LDS audience. It opens the door for Mormons to come to know a Jesus most readers will know little about—the Jesus of history." — David Bokovoy, author of *Authoring the Old Testament: Genesis–Deuteronomy*

"Meticulously documented and researched, the authors have crafted an insightful and enlightening book that allows Jesus to speak by providing both wisdom and council. The McConkies masterfully weave in sources from the Gospels, ancient and modern scholars, along with Christian and non-Christian religious leaders." — *Deseret News*

The story of Jesus is frequently limited to the telling of the babe of Bethlehem who would die on the cross and three days later triumphantly exit his tomb in resurrected glory. Frequently skimmed over or left aside is the story of the Jesus of Nazareth who confronted systemic injustice, angered those in power, risked his life for the oppressed and suffering, and worked to preach and establish the Kingdom of God—all of which would lead to his execution on Calvary.

In this insightful and moving volume, authors James and Judith McConkie turn to the latest scholarship on the historical and cultural background of Jesus to discover lessons on what we can learn from his exemplary life. Whether it be his intimate interactions with the sick, the poor, women, and the outcast, or his public confrontations with oppressive religious, political, and economic institutions, Jesus of Nazareth—the son of a carpenter, Messiah, and Son of God—exemplified the way, the truth, and the life that we must follow to bring about the Kingdom of Heaven.

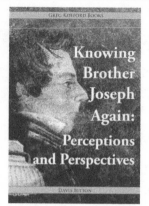

Knowing Brother Joseph Again: Perceptions and Perspectives

Davis Bitton

Paperback, ISBN: 978-1-58958-123-4

In 1996, Davis Bitton, one of Mormon history's preeminent and much-loved scholars, published a collection of essays on Joseph Smith under the title, *Images of the Prophet Joseph Smith*. A decade later, when the book went out of print, Davis began work on an updated version that would also include some of his other work on the Mormon prophet. The project was only partially finished when his health failed. He died on April 13, 2007, at age seventy-seven. With the aid of additional historians, *Knowing Brother Joseph Again: Perceptions and Perspectives* brings to completion Davis's final work—a testament to his own admiration of the Prophet Joseph Smith.

From Davis Bitton's introducton:

This is not a conventional biography of Joseph Smith, but its intended purpose should not be hard to grasp. That purpose is to trace how Joseph Smith has appeared from different points of view. It is the image of Joseph Smith rather than the man himself that I seek to delineate.

Even when we have cut through the rumor and misinformation that surround all public figures and agree on many details, differences of interpretation remain. We live in an age of relativism. What is beautiful for one is not for another, what is good and moral for one is not for another, and what is true for one is not for another. I shudder at the thought that my presentation here will lead to such soft relativism.

Yet the fact remains that different people saw Joseph Smith in different ways. Even his followers emphasized different facets at different times. From their own perspectives, different people saw him differently or focused on a different facet of his personality at different times. Inescapably, what they observed or found out about him was refracted through the lens of their own experience. Some of the different, flickering, not always compatible views are the subject of this book.

Common Ground—Different Opinions:
Latter-day Saints and Contemporary Issues

Edited by Justin F. White
and James E. Faulconer

Paperback, ISBN: 978-1-58958-573-7

There are many hotly debated issues about which many people disagree, and where common ground is hard to find. From evolution to environmentalism, war and peace to political partisanship, stem cell research to same-sex marriage, how we think about controversial issues affects how we interact as Latter-day Saints.

In this volume various Latter-day Saint authors address these and other issues from differing points of view. Though they differ on these tough questions, they have all found common ground in the gospel of Jesus Christ and the latter-day restoration. Their insights offer diverse points of view while demonstrating we can still love those with whom we disagree.

Praise for *Common Ground—Different Opinions*:

"[This book] provide models of faithful and diverse Latter-day Saints who remain united in the body of Christ. This collection clearly demonstrates that a variety of perspectives on a number of sensitive issues do in fact exist in the Church. . . . [T]he collection is successful in any case where it manages to give readers pause with regard to an issue they've been fond of debating, or convinces them to approach such conversations with greater charity and much more patience. It served as just such a reminder and encouragement to me, and for that reason above all, I recommend this book." — Blair Hodges, Maxwell Institute

Joseph Smith's Polygamy: Toward a Better Understanding

Brian C. Hales
and Laura H. Hales

Paperback, ISBN: 978-1-58958-723-6

In the last several years a wealth of information has been published on Joseph Smith's practice of polygamy. For some who were already well aware of this aspect of early Mormon history, the availability of new research and discovered documents has been a wellspring of further insight and knowledge into this topic. For others who are learning of Joseph's marriages to other women for the first time, these books and online publications (including the LDS Church's recent Gospel Topics essays on the subject) can be both an information overload and a challenge to one's faith.

In this short volume, Brian C. Hales (author of the 3-volume Joseph Smith's Polygamy set) and Laura H. Hales wade through the murky waters of history to help bring some clarity to this episode of Mormonism's past, examining both the theological explanations of the practice and the accounts of those who experienced it first hand. As this episode of Mormon history involved more than just Joseph and his first wife Emma, this volume also includes short biographies of the 36 women who were married to the Prophet but whose stories of faith, struggle, and courage have been largely forgotten and ignored over time. While we may never fully understand the details and reasons surrounding this practice, Brian and Laura Hales provide readers with an accessible, forthright, and faithful look into this challenging topic so that we can at least come toward a better understanding.

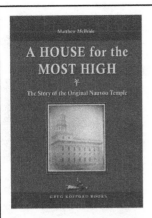

A House for the Most High: The Story of the Original Nauvoo Temple

Matthew McBride

Hardcover, ISBN: 978-1-58958-016-9

This awe-inspiring book is a tribute to the perseverance of the human spirit. *A House for the Most High* is a groundbreaking work from beginning to end with its faithful and comprehensive documentation of the Nauvoo Temple's conception. The behind-the-scenes stories of those determined Saints involved in the great struggle to raise the sacred edifice bring a new appreciation to all readers. McBride's painstaking research now gives us access to valuable first-hand accounts that are drawn straight from the newspaper articles, private diaries, journals, and letters of the steadfast participants.

The opening of this volume gives the reader an extraordinary window into the early temple-building labors of the besieged Church of Jesus Christ of Latter-day Saints, the development of what would become temple-related doctrines in the decade prior to the Nauvoo era, and the 1839 advent of the Saints in Illinois. The main body of this fascinating history covers the significant years, starting from 1840, when this temple was first considered, to the temple's early destruction by a devastating natural disaster. A well-thought-out conclusion completes the epic by telling of the repurchase of the temple lot by the Church in 1937, the lot's excavation in 1962, and the grand announcement in 1999 that the temple would indeed be rebuilt. Also included are an astonishing appendix containing rare and fascinating eyewitness descriptions of the temple and a bibliography of all major source materials. Mormons and non-Mormons alike will discover, within the pages of this book, a true sense of wonder and gratitude for a determined people whose sole desire was to build a sacred and holy temple for the worship of their God.

Modern Mormonism:
Myths and Realities

Robert L. Millet

Paperback, ISBN: 978-1-58958-127-2

What answer may a Latter-day Saint make to accusations from those of other faiths that "Mormons aren't Christians," or "You think God is a man," and "You worship a different Jesus"? Not only are these charges disconcerting, but the hostility with which they are frequently hurled is equally likely to catch Latter-day Saints off guard.

Now Robert L. Millet, veteran of hundreds of such verbal battles, cogently, helpfully, and scripturally provides important clarifications for Latter-day Saints about eleven of the most frequent myths used to discredit the Church. Along the way, he models how to conduct such a Bible based discussion respectfully, weaving in enlightenment from LDS scriptures and quotations from religious figures in other faiths, ranging from the early church fathers to the archbishop of Canterbury.

Millet enlivens this book with personal experiences as a boy growing up in an area where Mormons were a minuscule and not particularly welcome minority, in one-on-one conversations with men of faith who believed differently, and with his own BYU students who also had lessons to learn about interfaith dialogue. He pleads for greater cooperation in dealing with the genuine moral and social evils afflicting the world, and concludes with his own ardent and reverent testimony of the Savior.

For the Cause of Righteousness: A Global History of Blacks and Mormonism, 1830-2013

Russell W. Stevenson

Paperback, ISBN: 978-1-58958-529-4

**2015 Best Book Award,
Mormon History Association**

"In Russell Stevenson's *For the Cause of Righteousness: A Global History of Blacks and Mormonism*, he extends the story of Mormonism's long-standing priesthood ban to the broader history of the Church's interaction with blacks. In so doing he introduces both relevant atmospherics and important new context. These should inform all future discussions of this surprisingly enduring subject."
— Lester E. Bush, author of "Mormonism's Negro Doctrine: An Historical Overview"

"Russell Stevenson has produced a terrific compilation. Invaluable as a historical resource, and as a troubling morality tale. The array of documents compellingly reveals the tragedy and inconsistency of racial attitudes, policies, and doctrines in the LDS tradition, and the need for eternal vigilance in negotiating a faith that must never be unmoored from humaneness."
— Terryl L. Givens, author of *Parley P. Pratt: The Apostle Paul of Mormonism* and *By the Hand of Mormon: The American Scripture that Launched a New World Religion*

"You might wonder what a White man could possibly say to two Black women about Black Mormon history. Surprisingly a whole lot! As people who consider ourselves well informed in African-American Mormon History, we found a wealth of new information in *For the Cause of Righteousness*. Russell Stevenson's well-researched exploration of Blacks and Mormonism is an informative read, not just for those interested in Black history, but American history as well."
— Tamu Smith and Zandra Vranes (a.k.a. Sistas in Zion), authors, Diary of Two Mad Black Mormons

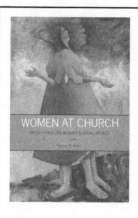

Women at Church: Magnifying LDS Women's Local Impact

Neylan McBaine

Paperback, ISBN: 978-1-58958-688-8

Women at Church is a practical and faithful guide to improving the way men and women work together at church. Looking at current administrative and cultural practices, the author explains why some women struggle with the gendered divisions of labor. She then examines ample real-life examples that are currently happening in local settings around the country that expand and reimagine gendered practices. Readers will understand how to evaluate possible pain points in current practices and propose solutions that continue to uphold all mandated church policies. Readers will be equipped with the tools they need to have respectful, empathetic and productive conversations about gendered practices in Church administration and culture.

Praise for *Women at Church*:

"Such a timely, faithful, and practical book! I suggest ordering this book in bulk to give to your bishopric, stake presidency, and all your local leadership to start a conversation on changing Church culture for women by letting our doctrine suggest creative local adaptations—Neylan McBaine shows the way!" — Valerie Hudson Cassler, author of *Women in Eternity, Women of Zion*

"A pivotal work replete with wisdom and insight. Neylan McBaine deftly outlines a workable programme for facilitating movement in the direction of the 'privileges and powers' promised the nascent Female Relief Society of Nauvoo." — Fiona Givens, co-author of *The God Who Weeps: How Mormonism Makes Sense of Life*

"In her timely and brilliant findings, Neylan McBaine issues a gracious invitation to rethink our assumptions about women's public Church service. Well researched, authentic, and respectful of the current Church administrative structure, McBaine shares exciting and practical ideas that address diverse needs and involve all members in the meaningful work of the Church." — Camille Fronk Olson, author of *Women of the Old Testament* and *Women of the New Testament*

CPSIA information can be obtained
at www.ICGtesting.com
Printed in the USA
FSHW022007190819
61227FS

9 781589 587267